Nudges

Nudges:
Thinking, Writing, Vocabulary, and Spelling

Paula Brock

Absey & Co.

"That is question now;
And then comes answer like an Absey book.
            King John, i, 9
                Shakespeare

ACKNOWLEDGMENTS

I owe a great debt to the teachers and writers who have preceded me; you will find many of their names in the Works Cited of each chapter.

I am truly grateful to my family—my mother, sisters, nieces, and nephews—but especially my husband Jim; my children Holly, Mike, Clint, and Rosalba; and my grandsons Seth and Isaac—for letting me be distracted, for completely slighting important occasions, for listening to ideas and drafts, for solving computer problems, for doing my chores, and for generally improving my spirits when I doubted myself the most.

This book would not exist were it not for the belief, encouragement, and great love of Joyce Armstrong Carroll and Edward E. Wilson. They are teachers' teachers. They are steadfast friends. They are positive thinkers. They are full of light and love.

And of course, I am thankful for the students who have patiently toiled away in my classes as I learned along with them the importance of teaching literacy in a rich and meaningful way.

>	Paula Brock
>	Georgetown, Texas
>	September, 2001

Cover photo by Edward E. Wilson
Design by Sarah Heiney

©2002 by Paula Brock

No part of this publication may be reproduced or transmitted in any form or by any means, electronic or mechanical, including photocopying, recording or any information storage or retrieval system, without prior permission in writing from the publishers.
Queries regarding rights and permissions should be addressed to:
Absey & Co., Inc., 23011 Northcrest Drive, Spring, Texas 77389. (281) 257-2340
Web site: www.absey.com
Published by Absey & Co., Inc., Spring, Texas.
Manufactured in the United States of America.

ISBN 1-888842-31-8

Foreword

Words. They are our business, our life lines, the building blocks of our thought and language. From the Biblical, "In the beginning was the Word..." to Winston Churchill's quip, "The short words are best, and the old words are the best of all," words affect us, define us, conjure memories, create excitement, lead us to understanding, and suggest history often as old as the paintings on the Lascaux caves. So when Paula made the commitment to write her book and invited my thoughts on a title, I said simply one word, "Nudges."

"Nudges," she replied trying the word out in her mouth, whisking it about a bit as one does a new flavor of ice cream or a familiar taste in an unfamiliar sauce. "Nudges." This time she spoke with a sense of finality. "I like it."

It is a proper title for a book that nudges teachers into ways to nudge students. It is a proper title because it, like the book's filling, it is of nuance yet directness. While denotations of *nudges* offer *poking* or *pushing*, *prodding* or *shoving*, connotations always lead to the word *gentle*. So there you have it, a book about gentling students into learning writing by a gentle but effective master teacher.

The word itself came into my academic consciousness when I heard Don Graves tell one of his stories about teaching writing. It seems he would carry index cards in his pocket. When he noticed something in a student's writing, he would take out a card and briefly write a NUDGE on it, something to keep the student going. I always liked that image: Student writing intently as the Master leans over and quietly places a note on the desk. No one around even notices the gesture–that simple act struck me as both personal and professional. That is exactly how I would describe Paula's book–personal and professional.

No accident decided the cover. Paula, with her years of experience as a horsewoman, often uses the analogy of working with horses (in the best sense of training them) to working with students (in the best sense of teaching them). Look closely at the cover, these magnificent horses running forever across the caves of Lascaux, perpetually engaged in nudging each other forward, form a perfect symbol of what awaits inside the book.

In her introduction, Paula encourages by assuring that she will stand beside you. I liken her rhetorical stance more to horse whisperer she often references. When you are finished reading her book and have internalized the strategies, you will continue to hear Paula whispering to you, gentling you into trying more, digging deeper. Her nudges will be both felt and heard because it is obvious that Paula Brock is the consummate teacher who believes profoundly in the students she teaches, the colleagues with whom she works, the teachers with whom she shares her profession, and in what she espouses.

–Joyce Armstrong Carroll, 2002

Preface

> "There is no cosmic importance to your getting something published, but there is in learning to be a giver. You have to give from the deepest part of yourself, and you are going to have to go on giving, and the giving is going to have to be its own reward."
>
> Anne Lamott,
> *Bird by Bird*, 203

I started on my journey as a writer with no expectations of ever publishing anything; I simply wrote for myself. Writing seems like such a natural extension of the teaching act, though, since teaching is about giving and giving and giving and then reaching to give just a little bit more; so somehow the decision to organize my thinking and put it on paper as a permanent gift to others took shape.

As I have taught over the years and now as I write to you, I am painfully aware of the small skill I bring to the task—how much I still do not know. I am such a late comer (late bloomer, you say?) to the compelling research on reading and writing! In the beginning, my research showed me how impoverished my knowledge was and how marginally prepared I was to teach language arts to anyone.

My reluctance to learn and resistance to change, however, turned to passion as I learned; during this stage in my development as a teacher, I managed to alienate a number of colleagues and even drove myself crazy at times. Further, I lived through some difficult personal times that served to temper me to reside more completely in my faith and to choose more deliberately a positive outlook. Then, as what I was learning and applying began to coalesce and make a fabric in my mind, I felt a jumping-up-and-down kind of joy like small children who are thrilled beyond words and create physical displays of their inward feelings. So I came to this grand idea of putting my thoughts into a small volume that might be a starting place for other teachers like me who love what they do but struggle to make a living, to make sense of the job, and to see a possible path through the labyrinth of pressures that play on modern educators.

Real writers will be smiling about now because this deprecating tone is as predictable as is the wee small voice that says, "Who do you think you are and why do you think anyone would want to hear any of your ideas?"

I know all about using invisible writing to quiet the critic who sits on the writer's shoulders; but I, of course, am fairly sure that my critic is speaking absolute truth and is just trying to save me from complete embarrassment.

Too bad, critic—go away! I am proud of these words and I have labored over them as a gift to any who might sit to read them and try to understand what is at work in the notion of literacy. I know that the ideas and strategies herein and the research that undergirds them are tried and true. These things work with students. I hope this will not be exactly the way I do things in my classroom next year; but I expect what I do then will go deeper, make more sense to all of us, and make the learning more accessible to my pupils.

School is a place that will always be asked to address the difficulties faced by the larger culture; school is a place that will always be asked to give and give and give.

It becomes more and more important to me as I work with students in the classroom that there is a deadly virus among us—a mental inertia. A speaker I heard last year posited that students were simply coming to us now from such a culture of material wealth that they expected to get by without any effort. There's obvious truth in that.

But maybe we in the education business have contributed by clinging to a system after the boat has clearly sunk. We hold on, for instance, to boring, repetitive drill and such an emphasis on getting the "correct" answer that we are all afraid to have an original thought. Students are both bored spitless and too constrained to take a risk; now there's a tension that ought to really enhance learning, don't you think?

I don't believe it's hopeless, however; I teach with too many intelligent, hardworking people who daily prove that they make a difference in the lives of the students privileged to learn from them. I have seen the spark of something learned light up the faces of too many students not to know good work is being done with them.

Here are some things you can do; look for manifestations of these ideas in the pages of this book:

- Establish practices and procedures that seem important to you; kids need predictable routine and structure to lessen the stress of living in the zone of proximal development.
- Figure out all you can about where each child is as a learner and what they need to learn. Teach from there.
- Try to devise the most concrete ways to present lessons that you possibly can.
- Make things easy and innovative.
- Manufacture ways to have fun.
- Reflect constantly on what you do.
- Make sure your students know you care about them.
- Gently nudge them along.

I will be standing beside you, cheering you on and wishing you well. There is no higher calling than to teach.

–Paula Brock

The First Nudge

THE FIRST NUDGE: PREWRITING

The Story

The first day of school is always full of excitement. Some students attend new schools; some make the transition from elementary school to middle school, or middle school to high school. Everyone's excited to see old friends or trembling inside to make new ones. The streets and highways are jammed with parents chauffeuring the youngest students to perhaps their first separation from home as well as the older students who can't yet drive themselves to school but are "entirely too cool to ride the bus."

I teach language arts—English. From the outside looking in, language arts seems like such a simple course. Most people think of it as having only two main components: reading and writing. So simple and so complex. If I consider only the issue of the range of reading skills of each individual student present in any one class, then I BEGIN to address the complexity of language arts for both the students and my teaching. But students can and do engage in this complexity every year, so the challenge then becomes how to invigorate the process—make it fun, enticing, nearly irresistible. Without such excitement, it is impossible to lure students to the cusp of learning. Students pass yet another year in school simply going through the motions, marking time—or worse: deciding that they are too dumb and too stupid to succeed in this school stuff.

The First Day

So—the first day—the first experience—is critical. The first day of school is the first experience students have under your tutelage, the first inklings they have of you as a person and a teacher, the first judgment they make about the course as to whether they can do the work, or if they might as well quit now because the class will be impossible. The first day sets the tone for all the days that follow.

Horse Sense

I meet every student at the door of my classroom with a handshake and a word of welcome on the first day. In *The Man Who Listens to Horses,* Monty Roberts uses the term "join up" to describe the relationship he's got to establish with a horse before he can teach the animal anything. Children are not horses, but principles that are useful in the world of nature often apply to nature's grandest creature. Teachers are sometimes given the advice "not to smile before Christmas." I'm not in any way advocating either a chaotic, anything goes classroom, or a buddy-buddy type of intimacy with students, but students need to know I want to be right where I am, and truly welcome them to join into study with me. (OK, OK, I know—summer was too short and inservice was too long, and if I were just luckier, I wouldn't have to work at all—but real is real, and the reality is that students need, in these times more than ever, teachers who give their hearts, their intellect, and their energy to them.) So I meet students with genuine pleasure that first day; offer them "join up," and keep offering "connection" to them for as long as it takes.

I ask students to purchase three plain, single-subject spiral notebooks (or something similar of their own choice) for my class. We christen one of these spirals WN, The Writer's Notebook. (I'll expound on that title and its meaning in chapter two.) One of these days "when my ship comes in," I'm going to have those spirals ready that first day for each student so that he or she can start with "the right stuff." For now, I'll have a few dollars' worth of spirals from the sales before school, plenty of notebook paper, and writing utensils available so that every student is able to participate in this first nudge into writing. I also provide colored, letter-sized file folders for each class; these can store our first day's writings and later become the collection folders for things like finished pieces of writing, metacognitive reflections, individual spelling word "walls", and portfolio assessments.

I have discovered through experience that it is better not to pre-label these folders with student names. A flurry of enrollment changes and schedule changes during the first two weeks of school—and lot sizes of 25 in a package of folders when I have classes of 26, 27, and 28 students—all conspire to waste expensive materials just by trying to have everything ready. Post-It Note® page markers make terrific name labels for the first week or two of school.

I can pass out books any old day. We can later decide together what our class guidelines need to be and what procedures work best for us for routine tasks. But first—IT IS IMPERATIVE—class has to be fun, and I want us to WRITE!

The Underpinnings

So how can I jump start student writers? Over twenty years ago, Janet Emig first described the reflexive mode of discourse in *The Composing Process of Twelfth Graders*. She suggests that the apt place to begin writing, although less familiar for most students, is from your own stories and knowledge. So, I set about looking for a stimulus so close to the *self* that all students would experience success. I wanted a stimulus that encourages the students who believe they can not write anything at all—or at least, nothing interesting or valuable or worth the effort. I wanted an idea that celebrates and affirms the lives and thinking and circumstances of all my students. I wanted a strategy as comfortable as an old shoe. I wanted a strategy from which I could scaffold so much more of the writing process as described in *Acts of Teaching*

(Carroll and Wilson). I wanted a strategy easy to do. The quickest and easiest thing I could think of was some sort of list, so why not name it after its predominant characteristics—quick and list – Quicklist?

Supplies

There is no need for exotic materials or intensive teacher preparation to write a Quicklist. Students use regular school notebook paper, and I make a simultaneous overhead transparency model or a butcher paper model which is displayed for each group.

The Strategy

First, students fold the notebook paper lengthwise down the red margin line at the left of the page, making a narrow vertical column. (Demonstrate as you give the oral directions). Then they make two wide vertical columns by folding the outside right edge of the paper in to meet the red left-hand margin line. (Tuck the outside right edge into the crease of the narrow vertical fold first made—much like tucking the edge under the flap of an envelope). Smoothing the paper back out after creasing these two folds, creates a narrow left-hand column and two wider but equal middle and right-hand columns on the page. (If students have their spiral notebooks, this folding/unfolding can be done with the pages still attached in the spiral; adjust your directions accordingly.)

Students begin listing at the top of the narrow left-hand column by entitling it NAMES. Going vertically down the page in that column, students write the first names, given names, or nicknames for:

1. Themselves and their family, listing one member's name per line (themselves, mother, father, sister[s], brother[s], and all steps);
2. Their grandparents and great-grandparents (both sides, living or dead, or they may pick ones they were close to);
3. Aunts, uncles, cousins (both sides and steps);
4. Dogs, cats, other pets, or favorite animals;
5. Vehicles (if the students' families do not name their cars, the students can simply write the model, color and year—"blue '57 Chevy").

If the lists run down and off the bottom of the page, I suggest students fold and start a second piece of paper. The Quicklist is easiest to use if it is written on only one side of the paper.
Continue listing:

6. hobbies, favorite pastimes, clubs, and activities (fishing, model airplane building, Scouts, 4-H, church, and others);
7. Favorite colors;
8. Favorite foods;
9. Two or three best friends.

Step Two
When the initial listing is complete, students return to the first name on the list, their own, and move horizontally across the page to the middle column. They label this column DESCRIPTIONS. Time spent brainstorming the kinds of things that might fill this column will be time well spent. Students tend to get into a rut in this section listing things like *nice* or *tall,* so the listing becomes an exercise in just getting this activity done. If the class first makes a list together, better specific descriptions are modeled that suit particular persons and things. For example, if the class collaborates on a description for "mother," characteristics will be suggested that either "connect" and make sense to students who are sitting there wondering what to write in the DESCRIPTIONS column; or, most students will realize and grasp the freedom they have to search for meaningful descriptions instead of certain "right" answers they think I want. (Besides, we humans are uniquely different yet amazingly similar at the same time; some whole-class brainstormed descriptions often fit several different people on several students' lists.)

To nudge, ask questions such as:

- What epitomizes Grandpa to you?
- Is Uncle John a Mr. Fix-it or a "Tim the Toolman"?
- Is your sister a college student or a newlywed?
- Had you better not let your dad run out of Dr. Pepper?
- What is Aunt Fluffy famous or infamous for?

Students might need help to think to include people's passions and occupations in their descriptions. Encourage them to list quickly whatever comes to mind; but lines can be skipped, thought about, and filled in later. Teach students that it is just fine to use ideas that others share with them. It is not cheating if they use descriptions from the class brainstorming that fit the names on their own lists; and it is perfectly acceptable to skip a name on the list, talk to someone at home, and then return to that name when there's more to say.

Making It Easy
Because of the time taken with the initial listing, the collection folder manage-

ment system, a minilesson on descriptions, and a class brainstorming model, the allotted time for class has flown by. Distribute 3"x 3" Post-It Notes® to students for additional names or additional information. One name per Post-It® gives the writer some space to write notes about that person, and then the Post-It's can be attached directly to the Quicklist without rewriting all the new information. If the expectation is for students to write A LOT, then at least try to save them from mindless and unnecessary copying!

Establishing the Reading/Writing Connection

It's important this first day to allow time to read a beautiful picture book like Patricia MacLachlan's *All the Places to Love* before going on to the third and final column of the Quicklist. The first reason it's important to share a book is that this gets the students up out of their chairs, moves them to a new seat around on the floor and changes their positions and perspectives. Second, this intimate setting, gathered together around each other with no desks or barriers, lays the first cord of the "bond ... created during a read-aloud that is unrivaled in terms of literacy ... until students experience that stage of their literacy growth, they can't move forward in their development" (Allen 45). Third, responding informally to a picture book parallels the naturalness of writing out of that book, not as an unrelated assignment with a pre-selected, correct response. Thus the connection between reading and writing is softly suggested.

Connecting Work to Life

Giving students a 3" x 5" Post-It Note®, I ask them to write a response to the book. We end class with a simple oral sharing by those willing to read what they thought. (Pick a book about memories, families, sharing, friendship—something that provides a visual feast as an added plus for this first experience of reading and sharing together.) Thus I establish a routine for the class—coming together for shared readings—but more importantly, establish the following ideas without actually voicing them:

- reading and writing are inextricably linked;
- writing is important and deserves time;
- good writing takes time;
- writing requires a willingness to return to it for review, re-thinking, and revision.

Continuing the Strategy

The second day, students add their Post-It Notes® to the names and descriptions they've already written, go back to the top of the list, and move horizontally over to the right-hand column. They entitle this column ANECDOTES.

I ask the class to define anecdotes and someone looks the word up for a literal, dictionary definition. One student scribes on the board as the class speaks. I am careful not to assume everyone knows what an anecdote is; do not to put anyone "on the spot" to define it who may not know the meaning, because embarrassing students on the second day takes six months to get them back—if ever. I might use a different term than *anecdotes* with young primary students, but even primary and intermediate students like big words if they're useful words.

Getting Hands On the Learning

Next, students draw a magic camera on an index card. Other teachers or relatives and friends may help assemble a collection of old cameras to have on display with some old black and white photographs. Judging from the amount of interest in something as simple as a few vintage primers I've collected and put on the front of my desk, having some props for lessons adds significance to those lessons and enhances students' ability to remember the lessons. They can take notes on this "camera" as you teach them Barry Lane's concepts of *snapshots* and *thoughtshots* from *After the End* (Lane 31-51). To summarize Lane, *snapshots* freeze moments in time via a magic camera that records not only light and shadow, images and color, but also the sounds, smells, and sensations of the moment. *Thoughtshots*, on the other hand, are like climbing to a high vantage point and looking down on a scene to gain perspective on the event and taking a picture. In other words, *thoughtshots* involve stopping to consider the big picture: the importance or significance of our experiences. Solicit from the class examples of each, and encourage students to write the word *snapshots* on one side of their magic camera, and the word *thoughshots* on the other. They may add any notes or examples for each that will help them remember how to access at least these two ways to think about stories.

Fig 1.1   Clair McLain

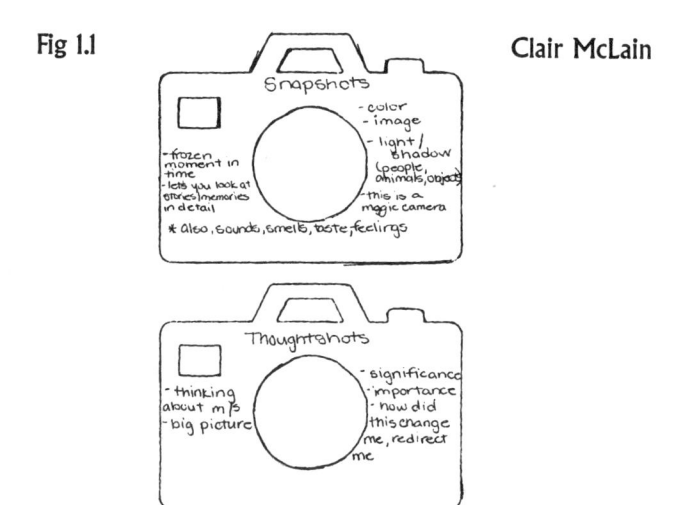

Snapshots
- color
- image
- light/shadow (people, animals, objects)
- frozen moment in time
- lets you look at stories/memories in detail
- this is a magic camera
* Also, sounds, smells, taste, feelings

Thoughtshots
- thinking about m/s
- big picture
- significance
- importance
- how did this change me, redirect me

The Importance of Modeling

In the anecdotes column, students condense their thoughts, ideas, and memories to key words and brief notes. I return to the transparency or butcher paper model and show how to generate questions for listing in this column. For instance, nudges might be:

> What is the best quality of your mom?
> Tell about a time you saw this quality in her.
> What does Dad like to do as a hobby?
> What is your favorite story about Grandpa?

As I write the anecdotes on my model list, I ask students to identify whether each is a snapshot or a thoughtshot. Then give an extended period of time for the students to work on the anecdotes column of their own Quicklists. Some students will not be able to write anecdotes on the spot for some of the names on their lists, either because they draw a blank and can't think of anything, or because they have forgotten the stories and connections they once knew. Sometimes they can't write anything because they truly don't know anything about that person. Regular 3.5 x 3.5 Post-It Notes® make it fun to do this as a homework assignment. Students write the names of those they need to find out about on the top of the sticky notes, one name per note. For homework, they talk to their family to get some anecdotal notes for each name. The next day, these Post-It Notes® can be applied directly to the blanks on the Quicklist—no recopying necessary.

Guiding Principles

Since all of us are better led by example, I send a powerful signal to students if I sit and write at this time, working along with my pupils. Actions speak louder than words; if I engage in writing myself, I know firsthand what is involved in the process. When I know from personal experience what students are up against as they try to write, I am much better able to help them over the hurdles they encounter.

Management Techniques

If students have been writing their Quicklists on loose paper, I ask them to tape or staple the pages into their WN, telling them that they never know when and where they might need an idea from the prewriting they've done. That way they have all this work somewhere where they can find it for future reference.

As an extension, they get a brad and two of those reinforcers for the holes in notebook paper. They punch a hole in the middle of the outside right edge of a piece of paper in their WN, and install their magic cameras in there, forming a pop-up, slide-out, manipulative effect.

No matter where students are as writers, wherever they are on a continuum from shut-down to fluent, they have in their Quicklist a rich repository of ideas. Further, unless I count the students' complaints that they've written so much their hands are tired, arrival at this point of plenty has been painless. (See Fig. 1.2)

STEAMBOATIN'

Discover Mark Twain's America.

It was a time of adventure. An age of grandeur. Mark Twain's Great Steamboatin' Era. Experience a past as much alive today as it was a century ago on a 2- to 12-night river vacation. For reservations contact your travel agent. For a *free* deluxe Steamboatin® brochure, return the coupon below or call any day of the week.

Red "Norcom"

Descriptions	Anecdotes
Fast paced, musical	Staying clean
Will always be there	Hardworking, thinking he has me
Loving, fast driver	Driving car over hump
Very tidy	Scared in public restroom
Relaxed, accident prone	Falling stories
Active, high energy	Trouble at school, car breaking down
Needs a break	
Doesn't care	Ungrateful Christmas
Musically inclined	Hospital visits
Busy	Arnie (dog)
Family man, tall, handyset	Dives into hot pool
Best Mexican food	Epilepsy
	Roosh w/sons & daughters
A little too loud	Embarrassed a lot
Scattered life	Softball bruise
A bit dingy, but ok	Bad Spanish
Young hunt	Indecisive about boyfriend
Smooth	Weddings (unusual)
Former runner	Hit by a car
Needs to be more responsible	Football games
Stable	Panics about injuries
Needs a little kind	Fights funny
Doesn't care what anyone thinks	Fighter
Scattered life	Fights
About 6'3" 290lbs	A bit of a bully
Skilled	Thought she could fix TV
Smart, country man	Spanish wedding

sharing, revising, and thinking has happened TOGETHER. This eem easy; and if one thinks something's easy, it is, in fact, easy. good friend Nancy Cahill taught my daughter to ride and work e used to say "make doing the right thing easy" and "the wrong horse. (Nancy Cahill has produced a number of American iation Youth Champions, Amateur Champions, and has ridden es to championships.) Just as the dancer cannot be separated e from my life, I say, "make doing the right thing easy" and "the

Paula Brock — Nudges

wrong thing hard" for students. If doing the right thing while learning seem easy, there's no limit to students' learning; if the doing is hard or confusing, then the lack of success students feel prevents learning. Worse still, confuse or force a student, and I SHOULD EXPECT balking or fighting back just like a young horse might do.

The Underpinnings

The Quicklist makes doing the right thing easy. In fact, from both the teaching and the learning perspective, the Quicklist has usability and durability precisely because it is so easy. Adaptable and naturally recursive; it can be added to, subtracted from, or tailored for any group of students at any level of writing competence. It is a non-threatening task, requiring no prerequisite academic knowledge or writing skill; it does not require elaborate preparation or exotic materials to produce rich results. The Quicklist is the softest of nudges; but it sends students a giant step forward because it encourages deliberate choice and purposeful thinking about writing. Some students tend to think of writing as just something they do and then see what happens, like rolling dice and hoping for sevens. They need to be empowered to go deeper and to dig more meaningfully into their own hearts and minds for something lasting from their educational experiences as readers and writers.

Scaffolding

Continuing to work to draw students into active participation and engagement with the learning process, I go to the board or overhead and ask them to help generate a plan of attack for an assignment. What I am actually doing is getting them to think out loud through a process; but what also happens is that they make a pathway for other students to use, students who may not have the foggiest notion of how to proceed from prewriting to writing and back again. I try to dissolve the mysteries surrounding the writing process by getting students to help each other. If students can orally express what they do when they write and how they do it, that gives the clueless ones just the nudge they need. (If we could hear their thoughts, I suspect we'd hear, "Oh! That! I see. Piece of cake.")

Putting Ideas to Work

After scaffolding, give students three or four colored, press-on stars or ask them to make a star with a marker, pen, or pencil next to three or four names on their Quicklists. These stars mark what they like or know best. I ask, "How would you go about developing a longer piece of writing about one of those names?" Predictably, students mention using:

    1. a web or a cluster;

2. further listing;
3. an outline (because this is the answer they think you want);
4. just take off and start writing.

Patience. I can't be afraid of blank looks and spaces of silence, or even of no responses. If students are entirely unused to responding from their own thinking to questions that have many possible correct answers, I may have to nudge them into an idea or two. If students offer no suggestions, I draw a web on the board, and ask students if they've ever seen anything like that. If no one has, I'll briefly describe it. If that minilesson doesn't generate any other ideas, I suggest they list thoughts and ideas about their starred names or simply jump in and start to write. Sometimes students can help describe what "listing" or "just writing" might look like. The important thing here are not certain specific answers, but rather the thinking and talking and sharing about how they go about the process of generating and developing ideas. Invite students to volunteer to model their strategies on the board or overhead. After several models are completed, we talk about the merits and drawbacks (if any) of each strategy. Use this discussion to lead into a lesson on invisible writing (Blau).

The Strategy

Each student needs a piece of carbon paper and a wooden skewer. They sandwich the carbon paper between two sheets of their WN, put a name from their Quicklist at the top, and use the skewer to write blindly on the top sheet. I tell students that it's no fair peeking to see what they've written; the idea is to write without worrying about grammar, spelling, sense or cohesiveness. (One tip that will help them keep up with where they are on the page as they write blindly is to use the index finger of their other hand to point to the line they're on as they write. This avoids writing over a line they've already written on.) They need three to five minutes for invisible writing, have them reread what they wrote, see if one or two students will share what they wrote, and talk about the activity—what surprised them, what they expected, how they view it as a prewriting activity.

Invisible writing is true freewriting as it helps students understand more easily how freewriting captures each thought without any concern for correctness. Freewriting has been called the mother of all prewriting techniques and likened to having a dialogue with the brain (Carroll and Wilson 66-67). Freewriting's use as mental aerobics is well-documented (Elbow 13-19). Freewriting's power ought to be obvious to us, who either because of education, training, or experience find if fairly easy to write on command. We do so precisely because we have learned how to turn the mind to a topic and think about it intensely. Freewriting for most students, however, is a pseudo-concept. Invisible writing helps students fully conceptualize freewriting and use the strategy in powerful ways to capture the thoughts that flit through their brains in that "brilliant, cosmic dance" (Barrett 19). (See Fig. 1.3)

Figure 1.3   Vickie Janda

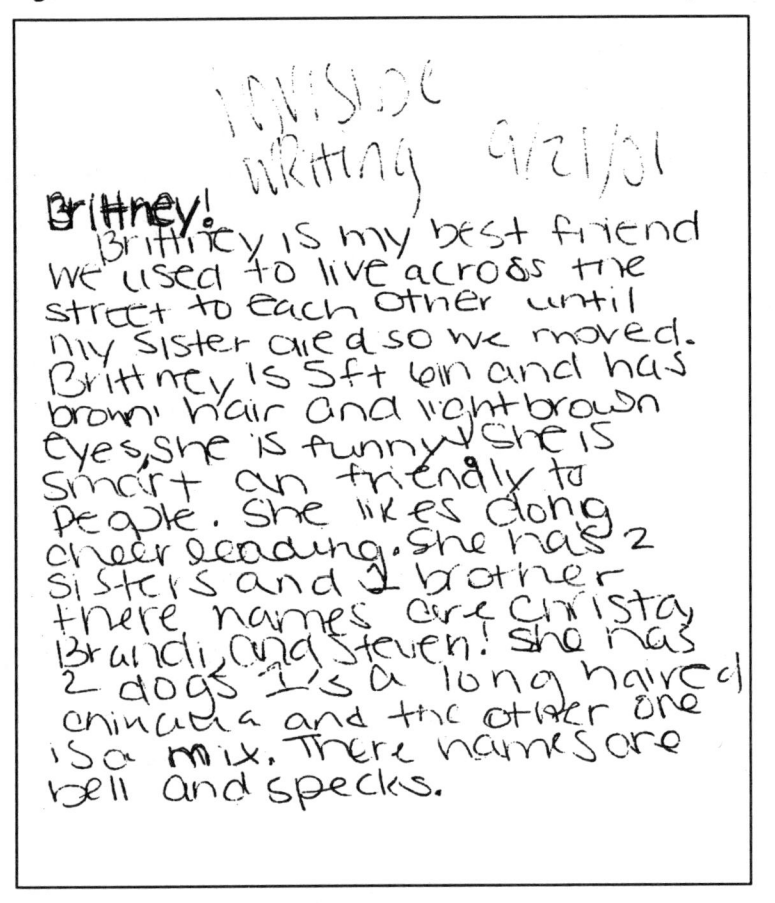

> Invisible writing 9/21/01
>
> Brittney!
> Brittney is my best friend we used to live across the street to each other until my sister died so we moved. Brittney is 5ft 6in and has brown hair and light brown eyes, she is funny. She is smart an friendly to people. She likes doing cheerleading. She has 2 sisters and 1 brother there names are Christa, Brandi, and Steven! She has 2 dogs 1's a long haired chiuaua and the other one is a mix. There names are bell and specks.

Do Something Different
    Invisible writing is effective because it is novel and allows students to discover for themselves the power of freewriting and how to use it to capture thoughts. Students more used to passive reception of information through film and video than the active genesis of thought sometimes act like they don't know they think—or at least, they don't think their own thoughts are worthy of consideration. To discover

they have active thoughts, introduce invisible writing which is also referenced in *A Community of Writers: A Workshop Course in Writing* (Elbow and Belanoff 11), and in *Families Writing* (Stillman 173). Stillman suggests writing with paintbrushes and citrus juice on paper that can then be read by holding the page over a light bulb. Another variation of invisible writing can be done on a computer by turning down the screen and then printing what was written. Either or both of these additional references will help students fully understand the point/purpose of invisible writing and choose a method of implementation that suits the circumstances of the assignment or interests of the writer. It is important to help students access the full concept of freewriting and replace their over-simplified idea that freewriting is just writing whatever they want—it's free. Revisiting freewriting using a variation listed above will ensure that students practice freewriting enough to give them ownership of it as a viable writing strategy.

Further Extension of the Strategy

Finally, students put each of the other two names they have starred on their Quicklist on the top of a clean sheet of paper in their WN—one name per sheet—and I show them how to use other prewriting strategies for each name. I usually use a web for one and Reporter's Formula (Carroll and Wilson 75) for another. If they can't think of anything for one name, they can switch to another name on another page. They may also add to their prewritings at home or any time they think of another description or story that fits their choices.

Evaluation

We are now three or more days into the first grading period of the school year. Students have completed a rather lengthy listing activity, an invisible writing, a web, and a Reporter's Formula for three names from their list. Students feel pride in the sheer amount of writing they've done, but teachers and students are still often driven and governed in many school districts by a certain number of required grades. Teachers have a curriculum to teach mandated by state and local education agencies; teachers are obligated to show student mastery of skills within a scope and sequence. Therefore, each teacher and/or each local district will devise a method to grade the body of work emanating from the first nudge. I give each day's activity 25% credit; four days equals one prewriting grade. The danger with this approach is the unstated idea students might get that prewriting is something they do first in writing and only first and that they never, ever go back to it during the course of writing. I combat this idea by continuing to introduce prewriting techniques/activities many times throughout the writing process. Another cumulative grade may be given by counting each of the three activities as 33% apiece. If I deal with highly reluctant students who have never experienced much success in the classroom, I may want to give a completion grade for each activity; some students need a real and visible reward for their efforts. I just make sure the approving remarks and interaction with each student doesn't get considered as cheap grades, grades they received like manna from heaven without any effort on their part.

Guiding Principles

This first nudge is important because it opens up writing both in the sense that it's the first writing experience, but also because it is an irresistible invitation to actually participate in writing. The Quicklist is also important because it acts as the genesis for writing ideas yet hidden in names, descriptions, and anecdotes. Because the Quicklist is a thinking tool, neither the students nor the teacher are at first fully aware of the ideas that might erupt from it. The Quicklist is also our in-house CPR system. Whenever we are blocked as writers, reading the Quicklist always revives us. And finally, the Quicklist is our security blanket against the great unknowns, the places and skills we will probe that we don't yet understand. The Quicklist is Home—Safety—Confidence.

WORKS CITED

Allen, Janet. *It's Never Too Late.* Portsmouth, NH: Heineman, 1995.

Barrett, Susan L. *It's All in Your Head.* Minneapolis, MN: Free Spirit Publishing Inc., 1992.

Blau, Sheridan. "Invisible Writing: Investigating Cognitive Process In Composition." *College Composition and Communication 34* (1983): 297-312.

Carroll, Joyce Armstrong and Edward E. Wilson. *Acts of Teaching.* Englewood, CO: Teacher Ideas Press, 1993.

Elbow, Peter. *Writing With Power.* New York: Oxford University Press, 1981.

Elbow, Peter and Pat Belanoff. *A Community of Writers.* New York: McGraw-Hill, Inc., 1989.

Emig, Janet. *The Composing Process of Twelfth Graders.* Urbana, IL: National Council of Teachers of English, 1971.

Lane, Barry. *After the End.* Portsmouth, NH: Heinemann, 1993.

MacLachlan, Patricia. *All the Places to Love.* New York: HarperCollins, 1994.

Stillman, Peter. *Families Writing.* Cincinnati, Ohio: Writer's Digest Books, 1989.

Roberts, Monty. *The Man Who Listens to Horses.* New York: Random House, 1996.

The Second Nudge

THE SECOND NUDGE: THE WRITER'S NOTEBOOK

The Story

Practice and experience are necessary components of human life. Children learn to walk and talk through practice and experience, and they certainly learn to sophisticate their language and communication by practicing and experiencing reading and writing. To learn to write fluently, aptly, and correctly requires frequent, dedicated practice; teachers have long understood that to achieve the amount of practice in writing that will be truly beneficial, students must write often. Writing in a classroom journal is often the assignment that seems the perfect answer to the need for this frequent practice; journals are easy to implement because they are fun, engaging, and productive for students.

But look inside. Examine what is really happening in classroom journals and the act of journaling. Am I and my students making the most out of the time spent writing in journals? Or is its regularity and lack of vitality degenerating journaling into a rote task devoid of life, energy and learning?

My solution is so simple that I wonder how I can coax a chapter out of the four principles I hold for journal writing: *write more often, write more variety, write more freely, and write with more help.*

Strategy 1: Write More Often

In a nine-week grading period on a block schedule (adjust the numbers to fit your district's time frame), I see each class of students 20 to 23 times. At a minimum, they need to practice their personal writing at least that many times within the grading period. So I assign twenty separate entries in their WN.

Most of my students' mouths drop at this assignment; they're convinced that I've just nudged them off a high cliff. However, I do want to raise the performance expectations to a high, academically challenging level. This is not a free grade with no rigor involved. This number of required entries is a high standard in the minds of some students; in fact, it is not nearly enough writing—twenty entries is less than one-third of the available sixty-three days in a nine weeks span.

Just remember, if twenty entries seems like a lot to students, it is vital that I pay attention to their perspectives rather than my own and not set the assignment number to an inappropriate level in their minds. I am cognizant of the fact that requiring twenty entries is not just throwing the gauntlet down, it is slapping them across the face with it. So I listen, I commiserate, and I encourage them to write about how frustrated they are and how utterly crazy they think I am. Just like playing baseball, no one gets extra credit for batting practice. The extra credit comes when the extra practice allows the batting average, earned run average, and home run record to rise. So it is with writing. Do more of it, and students' overall ability and confidence will improve. With practice, writing becomes easier and easier to do. It becomes more natural.

This is the perfect time to show students they have already completed five of the required twenty entries for this first term: they have a Quicklist, an invisible writing, a web, a Reporter's Formula, and a response to a read-aloud book. "It's not time to worry," I tell my students, "Because I'm going to help you get your entries, you will be able to help each other, and we will borrow ideas and stimulus from every resource we can put to work for us."

Making It Easy

I challenge students to lay aside every preconceived idea they have about writing journals; instead, I ask them to use this year's personal writing as both a laboratory to experiment with writing they've never tried before; and as a place to rest as with their oldest and best friend, recording the important things to them at these moments in their lives so the memories and ideas are not lost or forgotten.

Strategy II: Write More Variety

Like all creatures of habit, students will not just naturally write about different topics, attempt writing for varied purposes and audiences, or try different writing genres on their own. Water seeks the easiest path; so do I, and so do my students. The potential, to get stuck on certain topics and certain lengths of entries, to get into a deep rut with journals and not have anything to write about, seems to be the biggest problem I face with my students. These problems often destroy journaling before it ever gets established in the minds and hearts of student writers.

When students ask, "What do you want?" in their journal entries and "How long does it have to be?" I know they are trying to suck me back into doing all the thinking for them. It is as if, in Janet Emig's words, they want to write "from one layer of the self—the ectoderm only, with student involvement in his own thought and language moving down an unhappy scale from sporadic engagement to abject diffidence" (46). If students can get me to give them token daily topics and word or page limits, they develop a sense that it is not really important what they themselves have to say; they have neither a reason to write not any expressive drive to write. What I do, instead, is to give my students notes from books that have been written about journaling. For example, *A Writer's Notebook* (Fletcher) is loaded with possibilities such as suggesting that students write down what they wonder about (19), write down a human conversation (63), or write about artifacts, articles, quotes, or photographs (86-88).

The Importance of the Model

Models of writing for different audiences and purposes as well as different genres of writing should be done first as whole class activities, then as small group activities, and finally as individual activities. Simply teaching a brief lesson that tells what audience, purpose, or genre is will not do. Theory does not compute for every student; but if students employ text innovation or pattern a great writer, they try things they otherwise might refuse out of hand.

The Strategy

To experiment with audience, for instance, one way we start is to make a list together of as many different audiences as we can generate in five minutes or so; I do a talk through (really a think through) with the whole class about how my writing might change for different audiences. With their responses on the board or chart; we try some individual short bursts of writing on a single, simple topic, directing the writing each time to a different audience.

To address the purpose for writing, I have students consult a writing/grammar book for a discussion of the purposes writing serves, and then together generate a "gospel according to us" definition for purpose. They go back to the Quicklist (chapter 1) and find people, places, or ideas provoking writing topics that persuade, inform, tell a story, describe, relate to literature, or compare one thing to another, among others. As the teacher, I consider ahead of time what modes and purposes we need to cover specifically for the district's scope and sequence; I make sure to help students identify these specific types from their Quicklist. Students put all these notes and lists in their WNs so they have them as references to return to for reminders. There is enough variety available so neither I nor my students need ever be at a loss for providing the changes in direction that revitalize writing. Always looking for innovation and keeping variety and freshness in mind, bringing attention to these shifts and diverse approaches serves to stimulate students' thinking and the liveliness of their writing in the classroom. Energy must be present if I want students to do the reflexive writing that leads to real growth.

Strategy III: Write More Freely

The reflexive mode of writing seems largely ignored in public education; or, if it is addressed, it is considered creative writing and relegated to a narrow corner of the curriculum. If students always write for a specific task, with an assigned length and structure, and to a teacher-only audience, their writing becomes devoid of voice and life and meaning. To reclaim these wilted writers, to snare their interest, I help them open up and write more from themselves by tickling their minds with assignments for which there are no specific right answers. A boundless supply of trade and professional books help circumvent students' resistance to journal writing and make it easy to provoke response from them. I've tried something outlandish or avant-garde like a reading from *When You Lick a Slug* (Brown), or something designed to solicit response like the "playful ponderings" from *IS Your Bed Still There When You Close the Door?* (Healy). I can use the overused stubs and starters, but prefer fresh ideas like those from *Room To Write* (Goldberg) or *Conversation Pieces* (Nicholas and Lourie). Newspapers, magazines, and internet browsing bring current events to the consciousness; often what is happening in the world solicits responses from students because it is real and timely. Radio, television, and film are the media of choice among young people; so use these passions as springboards into writing.

Connecting Work to Life

My letter writing project (see Fig. 2.1) emanated from this type of

Fig 2.1

LETTER WRITING

EXPLANATION:
During the first week of each nine weeks' grading period, you will be responsible for writing a friendly letter to an adult who does not live here in Georgetown. You should explain in your letter that this is a school assignment worth a test grade and that you must get a response back from them in order to get your grade. It might be wise to give them a date to have a letter written back to you. The purposes of this assignment are many: to "make connections" with someone you care about, to practice the art of friendly correspondence, to write to "real" people for "real" reasons, and to engage in accountable and responsible activity in the language arts classroom.

DIRECTIONS:
1. The letters must be turned in already enclosed in a stamped, addressed envelope with your return address written in the top, left-hand corner of the envelope.
2. Turn this prepared letter in to me. I will *not* read the letters you send out, but I will give you a 100 daily grade for preparing the letter and turning it in to me for mailing.
3. When you receive a response, turn it in to me in the envelope it arrived in and I will give you a 100 test grade. (I respectfully request permission to glance over this reply to make sure it is going to provide you with the type of letter-writing experience I have come to expect.)
4. If your response is not turned in by the eighth week of the nine weeks' grading period, you will receive a test grade of 50 (because you will have fulfilled one-half of the assignment by sending the original letter).
5. There are measures you can take to ensure that you receive a response. Do the following:
   A. If after two weeks you have not received a response, write another letter to remind your relatives of the assignment. Mail this letter yourself; it does not have to go through the classroom.
   B. If, after four weeks, you have still not received a response, write a letter to someone new. Remember to explain the assignment to them. (You may decide to write to two new people at this step, to make sure you get at least one reply.)
   C. If, after six weeks you have still not gotten a reply, write reminder letters to everyone you have written and then write to one more different person.

TOPICS:
Write letters asking for information on a specific topic: do not bombard your relative with several topics. Ask for information about their daily life. Ask them about family, jobs, hobbies, or information on items you are interested in. Examples are: what mom/dad were like as children, the worst thing your mom/dad did as a child or a teenager, your favorite subjects in school, current events in society, and so forth. You should always include information about yourself and your immediate family members. Examples are: how you are doing, school events, social events, friends, extra-curricular activities, pets, etc. Make sure your letter asks for information so that they will have a reason to write back.

REMEMBER THAT YOU MAY ALWAYS CORRESPOND MORE FREQUENTLY THAN WHAT IS REQUIRED FOR YOUR GRADE, SO GET THOSE CARDS AND LETTERS FLOWING!!

thinking and continues to be one of the sweetest, so-glad-I-made-you-do-this assignments of my career. Students send and receive precious letters filled with love and wisdom and the pure pleasures of making new or deeper connections with people they know well or learn anew through this project. Reasons to write are much more evident to students after letters are exchanged. This writing for real reasons remains a powerful impetus to continue corresponding long after the assignment is finished.

Developing the Strategy
   I ask students to try some quiet, contemplative activities to stir the self to write. Taking students outside for five minutes of silent observation while they write down what they could taste, touch, hear, feel or smell renews their contact with, and wonder of, the natural world. (How many times do we look but not see?) The sense of smell, a powerful memory trigger, has students writing while conjuring up how the house smells when their favorite food is cooking. Or brainstorming aromas spark meaning and connection in their minds which leads to writing.

Extending the Strategy
   We are said to be a people who are dehydrated, sleep-deprived, and short of oxygen in these stressful days. *Writing Your Way Through Pain and Possibility* (Rico) contains some simple breathing exercises yielding written reflections on everything from air quality to a time when the writer may have been out of breath. *Re-creations* (Rico) is a book of technique for generating personal responses from and through poetry.

Establishing the Reading/Writing Connection
   Reading from children's books is THE WAY I foster deep, reflexive thinking because such books effortlessly lead readers and listeners into making personal connections with the story. I use everything from pre-kindergarten wordless books filled with intriguing pictures to books with ideas and subtleties sophisticated enough for adult tastes. First unfolded to me as reading-writing connections by Joyce Armstrong Carroll in her book *The Best of Dr. Jac,* I learned picture books spawn responses from students because the stories and pictures access the student's prior knowledge and experience and have application across other disciplines in the curriculum as well.
   Some students and teachers think picture books are too elementary and babyish to use; this viewpoint is simply uninformed. Such a view makes a negative judgment before experimenting with picture books. Some of the intangibles that may not be readily apparent to teachers who teach older students (nor to those students who consider themselves above such lowly activities) include the following:

- Picture books have limited text. This allows me to get in and out quickly with the idea, topic, genre or lead in toward which I am pointing.

- Picture books invite the eyes to feast on the images. Who can forgot what textbooks look like? They are dense with text and have few illustrations. Why not literally use the color and beauty and diversity of art mediums in picture books to create a welcome contrast to normal textbook fare?
- Picture books are sometimes in poetry but always in compact or compressed language. They say much within a short format. For this reason, they often lay the groundwork for a longer, more intensive piece of literature. Picture books are the seeds needed for the fertile fields of the mind.
- There are many picture books that are guaranteed to generate ideas that will be interesting for students to write about. I rarely miss this easy and different avenue to get writing started.
- When I get out from behind my desk and invite students around me on the floor, it is easier for them to focus their attention because of the intimacy of the gathering. One of the language arts addresses listening skills; what a painless way to help students listen more effectively. When I change my voice for certain passages in the books, students intrinsically learn things about reading comprehension; but they also see that I play and have fun. When I laugh or cry over a book, they see the power of meaningful text and the humanity of their teacher.
- Many picture books are so blatantly focused on reading skills like predicting and drawing inferences that it is unforgivable NOT to offer them as prompts for students.
- Big kids like pattern books as much as little kids do. The brain loves patterns.
- Reading aloud to students is an important component of a balanced literacy approach; while picture books are not the only things I read out loud, they are certainly the mainstay of my selections because of their availability and diversity.

There is no need to make working with students harder than it has to be or more boring than it has to be by dismissing a resource like picture books. Such trade books *will work* to free up student response.

Strategy IV: Write With More Help

Students do not come into my classroom already programmed with ideas, topics, and skills to use in their personal writing. It doesn't work to just tell students to write in their journals as if just voicing the assignment is all it takes to get substantive writing on command. In fact, many students have been doing the same type of journaling, responding to given cues, in so many classes they have strong negative reactions to such an assignment. It does work to approach the assignment WITH students, working hard to provide them the tools that will help them produce writings that have meaning, content and style—in short, writings that students are surprised and proud that they can do.

The Underpinnings

The best overall source of ideas and information for helping students with writing is *Acts of Teaching* (Carroll and Wilson) because it is a compilation of years of empirical research and the re-application and re-testing of theory and pedagogy with real writers and real students. This book provides teachers both an array of what to do to help student writers as well as why the given strategies work. Chapter three, for example, lists no less than twenty different prewriting strategies. Many of these strategies can be taught to students quickly, but the rhetorical strategies (76 and following) take more time and nudge students deeper into what they might write about after examining and thinking about literature, objects, and ideas. The rhetorical strategies offer heavyweight help to writers who then may use them as a bridge to thought.

Getting Hands-On Learning

The key to supporting students as they write is to make their first experience with a strategy or a technique as hands-on and experiential as possible. For example, when I teach the pentad as a help for writing, I draw a star on the board and label the points of the star with the perspectives Kenneth Burke established as the areas to explore in any drama: actors, actions, scene, agency (means), and motives (purpose). Then students draw big stars on over-sized yellow (what else?) paper, and I read a narrative picture book to them. I look for books that strike me as having strong characters who do things in their own ways for important reasons. Consider, for instance, *Amber on the Mountain* (Johnston), *A Day's Work* (Bunting), *The Bear and Mr. Bear* (Thomas), *Wodney Wat* (Lester), or *Lilly's Purple Plastic Purse* (Henkes). Students help me stretch with masking tape a large, free-form star on the floor after the story; then using the graphic on the board as a guide, they stand on the floor in or near the perspective that seems most important to them in the story. We talk about *why* they thought certain perspectives were powerful, and then they return to their tables to write about each perspective on each point of the yellow paper stars. I write, too.

Putting Ideas to Work

With a ruler, we join the points of the star to create the pentad shape, and I ask students to write in the spaces enclosed by these new lines. They write about how the points connect, interact, or influence each other. Afterwards, students take a broad-tipped marker and draw broken, dotted lines in a new shape around the perspectives that seem to them to go together. Time is given for students to freewrite their findings, using the ideas on the star points as well as in the connecting areas. In this way they delve deeper into the meaning and significance of the literature. Students like this activity because it is visual and tactile, but students also realize that generating a number of different thoughts and angles gives them much more to say about what they have read. (See Fig. 2.2)

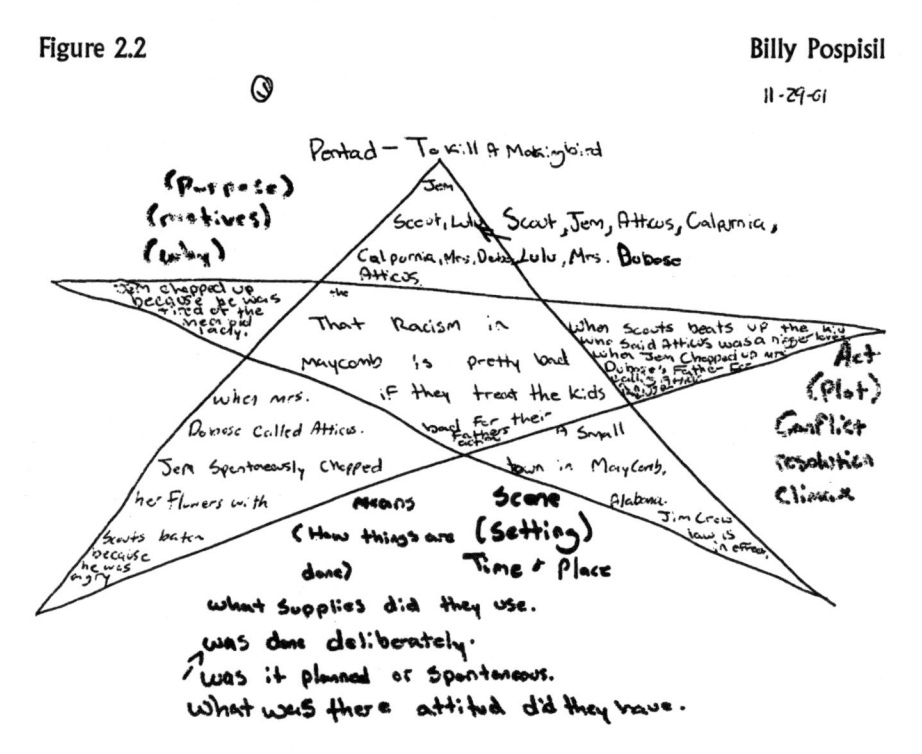

Figure 2.2   Billy Pospisil

Developing the Strategy
    Cubing (Carroll & Wilson 79) works similarly for writing about objects; classical invention (Carroll & Wilson 76) works for objects and ideas; and hexagonal writing (Carroll & Wilson 80) works for writing about literature, essentially introducing students to the methods of writing papers of literary criticism. Other professional books

also contain wonderful ideas that offer substantive help to student writers. *After the End* (Lane) gives two different ways to view events, as "snapshots" or "thoughtshots," for example. But nowhere under one cover is there another comprehensive collection of tried-and-true strategies like *Acts of Teaching*; nowhere else is there a collection of strategies that take students all the way through the entire process of writing.

Putting Ideas to Work

Students need a handbook to use to check their writing skills, and letting them write their own handbook in their WN is another effective way to nudge student writers into the help they need in order to write well and continue to improve. Minilessons can be done on active verbs, pronoun and antecedent agreement, complete sentences, combining sentences, paragraphing, and common usage errors. Notes on such grammar topics as these give students a readily available resource to consult to answer the correct usage questions they have as they write. Sometimes students will not revise their writing or correct errors simply because it is too much trouble to go and look in a grammar book; having an easy reference familiar to them helps alleviate this problem.

The Underpinnings

I find I teach more grammar to students than ever before when I truly teach students to write; however, the grammar instruction produces better results because of its timing (lessons are taught when students need them) and because it is contextual (students see the grammar at work in the reading and writing they are doing). A number of Aristotelian, experiential books have been published in the last few years that have helped me teach grammar minilessons to students—with the notes and models going into their WN as authentic grammar guides. Four examples of such resources are *Minilessons for Revision* (Geye), *Elementary Minilessons* (Ramos), *Mrs. Myrtle Frag, the Grammar Nag* (Bailey), and *Grammar in Story* (Windsor); I found it a waste of time looking anywhere else for lessons more compact, ready-to-use, and apropos to the needs of writers.

One final way I help students is to teach them about the different *types* of journals by experimenting with different modes of journaling within the WN. *Journaling: Engagements in Reading, Writing, and Thinking* (Bromley) is a quick, uncluttered synopsis of different kinds of journals. Bromley lists purpose or point of view journals such as present day journals, fantasy journals, journals from the past, travel journals, or science journals, for example. She describes literature response journals, learning logs, dialogue journals, buddy journals, double-entry journals, and others. Every one of these approaches has merit. A common mistake is zeroing in on only one type of journal or one purpose for journaling, and never giving students any help, guaranteeing this assignment will go stale with both students and their teacher. Any one WN approach limits if it is taken as an absolute in and of itself. Using only one approach to journaling narrows the scope and disconnects and compartmentalizes the writing too much to let it be powerfully at work in the intellect and psyche of students.

The Connection to the Individual

We take the time during class to personalize the cover of WN. I ask students to draw their eyes, or their face with their eyes, on plain manila card stock, cut this out, and paste it on the inside front cover of their WN. We spend a lot of time in the WN; we use the image of the organs of sight and the individuality each student gives to the rendering of his or her face and eyes as a metaphor for the re-seeing, second sight, hindsight, and insight I hope to stimulate for each student through his or her work in the WN.

Establish Clear Expectations

We also brainstorm a list of rules and requirements to govern our writing. The requirements I submit are:

1. every entry be dated;
2. every entry, even if it is doodling, drawing, or attachments, should be accompanied by writing.

Students usually suggest:

3. writers skip a few lines between entries, and
4. absolutely-not-to-be-read entries may be signaled by folding the paper across the page in a triangle.

The Underpinnings

I do not read my students' journals unless I am asked to read something or unless I think there is a student in danger of hurting himself/herself or others. I am always honest with my students and their parents about this issue, so I do make it clear I *must reserve the right to read* the journals if I think a student is somehow in jeopardy. However, I fully expect not to read these reflexive writings. There are convincing arguments to be made for the needs students have to their own privacy, especially a place where it is safe to explore ideas and thoughts through writing.

Experts also write about the field of force that the audience exerts on the writer, creating a pull and actually affecting thought. I put it this way: students need to be allowed to engage in their own processes. I encourage them to leave the sit-there-in-the-desk-and-be-filled paradigm and actively engage in their own learning. If they are always writing for me, the teacher, they will be limited by what they try and what they learn because they focus on what they think I want them to say.

Cautions

In the research literature regarding journal writing, there are strongly differing opinions on the issue of not reading student journals. To name two: There is the issue of legal liability, and there is the danger of writing that is done for the writer's eyes only creating an incomplete picture of the writing process and overall literacy. I compensate for these difficulties by conferencing with students, setting up opportunities for them to buddy-journal and share with each other some of their journal entries, using the WN as the source for pieces of writing that are polished and brought out into the public domain, and asking students to reflect on their WN by writing to me about meaningful and successful passages.

Making It Easy

Through the WN, I nudge students carefully down a path that allows writing fluency to develop driven by a student's own burgeoning interest in the process of writing. I nudge them down a path that allows the twin capacities of skills and meaning to meet as students discover their own potentialities and motivations for doing the assignments. Because I protect my students by NOT reading and responding to every single word they have written, they have nothing to lose and everything to gain by trying. Because I have protected myself from the dreaded marathon grading sessions for student journals, I have the energy and the passion to offer fresh and varied writing experiences and continued encouragement for my students as they engage in real writing. I have the mental sharpness to suggest appropriate options and choices when we conference. Because I have relinquished my control of the students' journal writing, they have the opportunity to make choices themselves and reflect upon the results.

The Underpinnings

Process is not something you can do to someone else. My students do not need a teacher who is trying to micro-organize and orchestrate their thinking and the products of their thinking. My students do not need a teacher who is so stressed from reading student journals she can't think straight and is grumpy, resentful, and frustrated. What my students need is for me to stop trying to apply external motivation to get them to do substantive work. They need me to back off, open possibilities to them, give them little nudges, and then watch in open amazement as they began to learn *through* the writing. This is not a quick process, but it is a powerful and empowering one. While I have understood the theory of process for years, I did not understand how potent and organic it was until I began to let go of the control of students' journals in my classroom.

Evaluation through Metacognition

I evaluate the results of each student's work in his or her WN through simple five question overviews (see Fig. 2.5). Most students grade themselves fairly in these reflections, and this type of evaluation has the benefit of getting the students to contemplate what they are doing, and what they need to do, as learners.

WRITER'S NOTEBOOK REFLECTION

Please answer the following questions as fully and completely as you can. Write from your heart and with your clearest thinking as you consider and respond to each question.

1. How many entries do you have in your Writer's Notebook for this nine weeks?
2. What types of entries do you have (assignments, notes, remembrances, etc.)? Do you think you have fulfilled the requirements of having different types and different lengths of entries? Explain.
3. Which entry do you think is your best entry in this grading period? Why do you think it is your best entry? Lift a portion of that entry out of your notebook and copy it down in your reflection – it does not need to be long – only a sentence or two will be fine. What do you think this excerpt of your writing shows about you?
4. Keeping in mind that twenty entries divided into a grade of "100" makes each separate entry worth five points, what grade would you give yourself for your Writer's Notebook this nine weeks? Have you done the best work you can do on your Writer's Notebook? Why or why not?
5. Tell me one specific thing you learned from doing the WN. Why do you think you learned that specific thing?

Fig 2.5

Horse Sense

While training young horses, it soon became obvious that I could teach the horse what I wanted him to do if I could coax some movement out of him. I had to get the horse to stir out of his tracks and move. It didn't matter if he got excited or moved quickly or danced all around; I could do something with movement. If he balked and refused, I couldn't teach him a thing. Further, a balked animal is as dangerous as a coiled spring; he's wound tight, and when that energy is released, I don't want to be in its path.

Guiding Principles

Teaching kids to write works exactly the same way. If I can get them to try any little movement at all towards writing will do I can teach them until the making of meaning through writing takes hold of them and pushes them forward without me.

WORKS CITED

Bailey, LaWanda. *Miss Myrtle Frag the Grammar Nag.* Spring, Texas: Absey & Company, Inc., 2000.

Bromley, Karen. *Journaling.* New York: Scholastic, 1993.

Brown, H. Jackson, Jr. *When You Lick a Slug, Your Tongue Goes Numb.* Nashville, Tennessee: Rutledge Hill Press, 1994.

Bunting, Eve. *A Day's Work.* New York: Clarion Books, 1994.

Carroll, Joyce Armstrong. *The Best of Dr. Jac.* Spring, Texas: Absey & Company, Inc., 1998.

Carroll, Joyce Armstrong and Wilson, Edward. *Acts of Teaching.* Englewood, CO: Teacher Ideas Press, 1993.

Emig, Janet. *The Web of Meaning.* Portsmouth, NH: Boynton/Cook Publishers, Heinemann, 1983.

Fletcher, Ralph. *The Writer's Notebook.* New York: Avon Camelot, 1996.

Geye, Susan. *MiniLessons for Revision.* Spring, Texas: Absey & Company, 1997.

Goldberg, Bonni. *Room to Write.* New York: A Jeremy P. Tarcher/Putnam Book, 1996.

Healy, Jane M. Ph.D. *Is Your Bed Still There When You Close the Door?* New York: Doubleday, 1992.

Henkes, Kevin. *Lilly's Purple Plastic Purse.* New York: Greenwillow Books, 1996.

Johnston, Tony. *Amber on the Mountain.* New York: Puffin Books, 1994.

Lane, Barry. *After the End.* Portsmouth, NH: Heinemann, 1993.

Lester, Helen. *Hooway for Wodney Wat.* Houghton Mifflin Boston, 1999.

Lowrie, Paul and Bret Nicholaus. *The Conversation Piece.* New York: Ballantine Books, 1996.

Ramos, Jodi. *Elementary MiniLessons.* Spring, Texas: Absey & Company, Inc., 2000.

Rico, Gabriele Lusser. Pain and Possibility. New York: A Jeremy P. Tarcher/Putnam Book, 1991.

_____. *Re-creations.* Spring, Texas: Absey & Company, Inc., 2000.

Thomas, Frances. *The Bear and Mr. Bear.* New York: Dutton Children's Books, 1994.

Windsor, Lucinda. *Grammar in Story.* Spring, Texas: Absey & Company, Inc., 2000.

The Third Nudge

The Third Nudge: Vocabulary

The Story

Words are the means by which we do language arts. Words may be called the currency of communication; words are the meaningful units by which we read, write, speak and listen. Acquiring a broad and rich working vocabulary is part and parcel of education and often seems to be the pivotal point at which readers either develop or do not. When every word is hard to read, regardless of whatever skill is missing for that student, the struggle can simply be too much—the student gives up.

So every language arts teacher feels compelled to teach vocabulary, thinking that perhaps if we give students ownership of more words, maybe reading will catch on with them, that some level of accomplishment will light the fires making them hungry to read, and then reading will become its own driving force. Parents also expect teachers to teach vocabulary because they studied vocabulary lists in school, and "if it was good enough for them. . . . " School boards and curriculum directors expect teachers to teach vocabulary "because students need formal vocabulary instruction to prepare for standardized tests that have advanced vocabulary components." Students and teachers alike feel the pressure to learn vocabulary because they realize that vocabulary acquisition and progression builds upon itself and that comprehension is at stake.

The Underpinnings

Educators know that the best way to build vocabulary is to be immersed in a print-rich environment: to read widely and often. But thoughtful, reflective teachers begin to worry when they realize that for many different and complicated reasons, too few students read widely and often. It seemed obvious to me that SOMETHING NEEDED TO BE DONE to remediate and support students when they tried to read but found themselves short of the tools necessary to comprehend what they were reading—when they realized they needed a richer vocabulary.

Observed Student Behaviors

In my school, the phrase I would sometimes hear is "Am I bad?" to cover students' embarrassment at their lack of knowledge of how to call certain words or how to decipher the meaning of the words they could call but did not understand. Many students nowadays will openly express frustration whenever a passage does not make sense to them by remarking "This is stupid," and refusing to proceed. I myself will stop reading, too, when I can't make meaning from the words of a text; but I have the interest, skill, and discipline to attack and solve such comprehension problems.

Just like students, I do feel the difference in pace and motivation to get reading done that I have *assigned* myself to do, especially if that reading is academic or scholarly—challenging because of its vocabulary and syntax. If I feel this myself and love to read, what can I do about the same feelings magnified ten-fold for students who tell me they hate to read and seem to avoid reading at any and all costs?

The Strategy

I wanted a system of studying vocabulary that would be student-driven, simple to operate, and connected and integrated with what students and I were required to do for class. I wanted students to manipulate words in all kinds of ways; I wanted the words they had to study to be meaningful to them individually and help form patterns and connections in their brains. I wanted vocabulary study to be fun and on the very edge of students' capabilities.

Locating Words for Study

The first problem in acquiring vocabulary outside the act of reading itself is to settle upon a list of words for dedicated study. I used to do the expected thing: I gave students a list of words for each literary selection, they would define them and sometimes write sentences for them, and then they would take a vocabulary test. Most students would request to review the words for about ten minutes before the test, ace the test, and then go merrily along their way with the words forgotten as soon as their bodies cleared the door.

When I began to grade myself on what I was doing with vocabulary in the classroom, I found I fell far short of what I considered meaningful work. I also didn't think my colleagues who reported astonishing results studying things like SAT words lists in isolation were really doing any better. Were students learning useful and appropriate words? Did newly acquired vocabulary show up in students' actual use, in their speaking and writing and love for reading? Did students have the sense that their vocabularies were improving? Did students know that reading was easier and more meaningful because they comprehended more of the words? Was there any statistical proof that new vocabulary words were retained over time?

Since I had to answer *no* to these questions, it was time to abandon my old practices and try to find some answers to the question of how to make learning vocabulary more *accessible* to kids. In particular, it was time to remove myself as head honcho of words and put students in charge of their own vocabulary improvement. "...there is no such thing as teaching—only learning. Knowledge...must be pulled into the brain by the student, not pushed into it by the teacher. Knowledge is not to be forced on anyone. The brain has to be receptive, malleable, and most important, hungry, for that knowledge" (Roberts 87-88).

There does, however, need to be some structure, some method, for students to follow; so my job was to come up with the means to study vocabulary words where students were meeting them—in their reading.

Materials Needed

Simple, inexpensive, and easy to keep up with materials were also a priority; if students lost their word lists, it set them up for failure and stopped any possibility of learning dead in its tracks. I decided to use both colored and white lined index cards and provide students a two inch, snap-apart, metal binder ring to hold the cards together. Students brought in the cards and also supplied inexpensive hole punchers; I kept these supplies in my room so that they were not subject to being left at home, forgotten, or in the wrong folder.

Our vocabulary work consists of three parts. The first part, a collection vehicle, I dubbed *Vocabulary Bookmark Cards* (VBC). The second part, a selection and study vehicle, I called *Vocab Grab Cards* (VGC). The third part, a manipulation vehicle, I called *Vocabulary Activity Pages* (VAP). The VBC uses colored index cards, the VGC, white index cards, and the VAP are copies provided by me which students use as patterns/templates on regular notebook paper. The VAP's go into students' Vocabulary and Spelling Spirals. In this way, students easily organize their work and keep up with it. I ask students to bring their cards and their Vocabulary and Spelling Spirals to class just like textbooks. Like the WN, I consider these notebooks essential materials for our work together.

The Strategy: Vocabulary Bookmark Cards

For VBC (see figure 3.1), students learn how they go about the work of collecting vocabulary words they do not know. I define words they do not know as words they might get an inkling of, or most of the meaning of, in the sentence just by the context of what was being said; but, they cannot take these words and use them correctly in their speaking and writing. I also suggest these are words students have seen before and run into while reading but do not feel they are words they own.

Fig 3.1

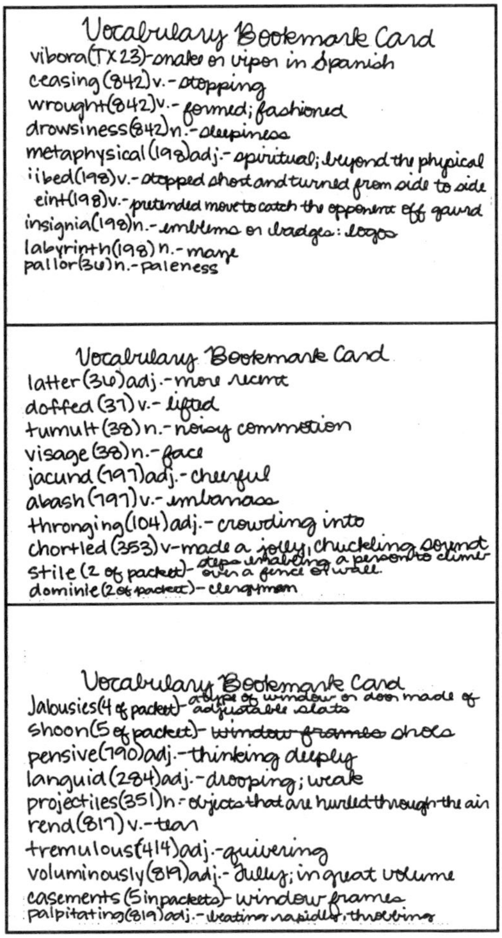

```
Vocabulary Bookmark Card
vibora (TX 23) - snake or viper in Spanish
ceasing (842) v. - stopping
wrought (842) v. - formed; fashioned
drowsiness (842) n. - sleepiness
metaphysical (198) adj. - spiritual; beyond the physical
ibed (198) v. - stopped short and turned from side to side
feint (198) v. - pretended move to catch the opponent off guard
insignia (198) n. - emblems or badges; logos
labyrinth (198) n. - maze
pallor (30) n. - paleness
```

```
Vocabulary Bookmark Card
latter (36) adj. - more recent
doffed (37) v. - lifted
tumult (38) n. - noisy commotion
visage (38) n. - face
jocund (797) adj. - cheerful
abash (797) v. - embarrass
thronging (104) adj. - crowding into
chortled (353) v. - made a jolly, chuckling sound
stile (2 of packet) - steps enabling a person to climb over a fence or wall
dominie (2 of packet) - clergyman
```

```
Vocabulary Bookmark Card
Jalousies (4 of packet) - a type of window or door made of adjustable slats
shoon (5 of packet) - window frames shoes
pensive (190) adj. - thinking deeply
languid (284) adj. - drooping; weak
projectiles (351) n. - objects that are hurled through the air
rend (817) v. - tear
tremulous (414) adj. - quivering
voluminously (819) adj. - fully; in great volume
casements (5 in packets) - window frames
palpitating (819) adj. - beating rapidly; throbbing
```

Sarah Marriott

To create VBCs, students either interrupt their reading to jot down these words and their page numbers; or they read a page, a chapter, or a story, getting a sense of the meaning, and then reread and record the words and page numbers. Students work on the lined side of the colored index cards. They record a word and page number per line, skip lines per entry, or set the pattern of recording in a fashion to suit themselves if they had a bold, sprawling type of handwriting or wanted to do something unique and artistic.

Later, students look up each word on their VBCs in the dictionary, write a brief definition for each, and then use the page number to go back and read the word in its original context. This is the appropriate and meaningful time to do some dictionary work where we look at words with multiple meanings and practice how to determine the meaning for these words as they are used in whatever we are reading.

Management Technique
Some kind of identification information is necessary for the back of each card. I find that the student's name, class period and a grading period are usually enough to minimize loss and confusion and maximize the ability to locate the word again in its original context. As each VBC is filled, a hole is punched in it and the card is strung on the metal ring. Once begun, VBCs are kept throughout the school year on every type and piece of literature read. I require that students find *a minimum* of 50 words for VBCs each nine weeks, they count the words defined with page numbers, and I multiply that number by two for a test grade. This is a substantive amount of dictionary work, and I want to honor that hard work with a substantive grade.

Words to Avoid
There are some words that I do tell students to exclude from VBCs:

- words that are place names or proper names
- words that are archaic, dialectic, or meaningful only for that one text (This last is a tricky ban and you'll have to help students by modeling to discern which vocabulary words to pull that are broader and not so limited or particular in use.)

The Strategy: Vocab Grab Cards
Enough vocabulary words from reading should be collected on VBCs after the first week of school to begin part two of this project: Vocab Grab. In part two, students will grab five words from their VBCs and transfer them to white, lined index cards. It is a good idea to spend some time at this point talking about *Hefty, Hefty, Hefty* words so that students pull out the most widely applicable, useful words they can; one of the things my students and I recently realized is that if the words they grabbed from their VBCs did not have synonyms and/or antonyms, they were probably too narrow in meaning to pull out and study. Examples that fit this category that were pulled out this year were words like *flivver, dell,* and *smilax*—all words that had only one meaning and were not necessarily going to be widely found in reading. These were great words for VBCs because they broadened students' knowledge, but they were not words with the kind of frequency and rich meaning in reading that would make them the best choices for dedicated study.

On the unlined side of the white VGCs, students print the vocabulary word they chose in large, legible letters like a flash card (see figure 3.2).

Fig 3.2

```
✶                              ✶

        Entity
        s= self-contained
        a= dependant



        Imprudent
        s= insolent
        a= shyness, conservative


     vocab. Grab cards
        ✶                      ✶

        Tumult
        s= commotion
        a= peace
```

Underneath this printed word, students write one synonym for the word and one antonym for the word.

Turning the card over and using its lined side, students write the same identification information they used on their VBCs, copy the definition of the word from their VBC, write the pronunciation guide for the word (there's not much point learning a vocabulary word you can't then pronounce), and then copy the sentence where they found the word in its original text.

Five words *grabbed* from each individual student's VBCs are studied every two weeks. To study, students read their five VGCs every day for a week, write their words down in their vocabulary and spelling spiral, and take a mock test on their own while I am checking roll or at some other appropriate time when they are directing themselves during class.

Connection to Life

Inform parents about these vocabulary projects at the beginning of school by letter and again at Open House. In my district, parents attend all their child's classes for five or ten minutes each on a given evening. I encourage parents to get involved in their students' study by holding up the flash cards (the white index cards) and drilling their students at home; or, they might use their child's study words in family games or conversations.

The Story
I had used VBCs and VGCs for about two years when I began to suspect that students were just going through the motions of vocabulary study. Somehow I had to get them to THINK about their words. Even a limited amount of research about vocabulary acquisition clearly showed me that "it takes more than definitional knowledge to know a word, and we have to know words in order to identify and use them in our own speaking and writing" (Allen 8). So, although we'd spent quite a lot of time pulling, defining, and going over words, that work merely formed the foundation for LEARNING those words. That's when I added the Vocabulary Activity Pages (VAP) component.

The Underpinnings
Words, Words, Words by Janet Allen is my current right hand resource for vocabulary because it strains the research on the teaching of vocabulary clearly into what works and what doesn't, and also because it gives strategies, techniques, activities and ideas from which to build vocabulary experiences for students that will be effective in developing their understanding and repertoire of words.

Many of us who currently teach language arts were taught *content* not *process*. We were just pointed towards word lists and expected to learn those words by exposure or osmosis or some sort of magic. Later on as teachers, we learned to invoke the handy little phrase learning new words contextually in our conversations about vocabulary instruction so that it sounded like we knew what we were talking about. I didn't. I think I just thought that somehow students would develop a full, rich meaning for words from the context around those words—every time. This over-simplification did not deal with the problem of some texts being so complicated that the words *around* the unknown word were also unknown to the readers; nor did it explain how readers get a sense of what words mean without being able to precisely define the word they just read.

In fact, a person who is a reader and can't remember not being a reader finds it hard to explain how they know the vocabulary words they know because those words were seldom directly taught. That's the result of reading widely and often. Allen's book gives us a place to start with students who are not reading widely and often. She details her experiences, thinking processes, research and lessons in such a way that they are accessible directly from the book so that students may use them.

The Strategy: Vocabulary Activity Pages

During the first few weeks while students are collecting their first words and learning the formats of VBCs and VGCs, I do minilessons using various graphic organizers from Allen's book to show students how to manipulate their VG words. We use an Analysis Map (135) because it is so easy for students to start with the synonyms and antonyms they already have on their VGCs and continue comparing and contrasting on the Analysis Map (see figure 3.3). We use a Context-Content-Experience (136) organizer because it is so important for students to be aware of what using the context actually means and to practice using the context for word meanings; and it is also important to connect reading to personal experience. Both skills are inherent in this page (see figure 3.5). We use a Linear Array (137) because it is short and resembles webbing (see figure 3.4). This graphic organizer also gives kids a range of meaning for words that deepens their understanding.

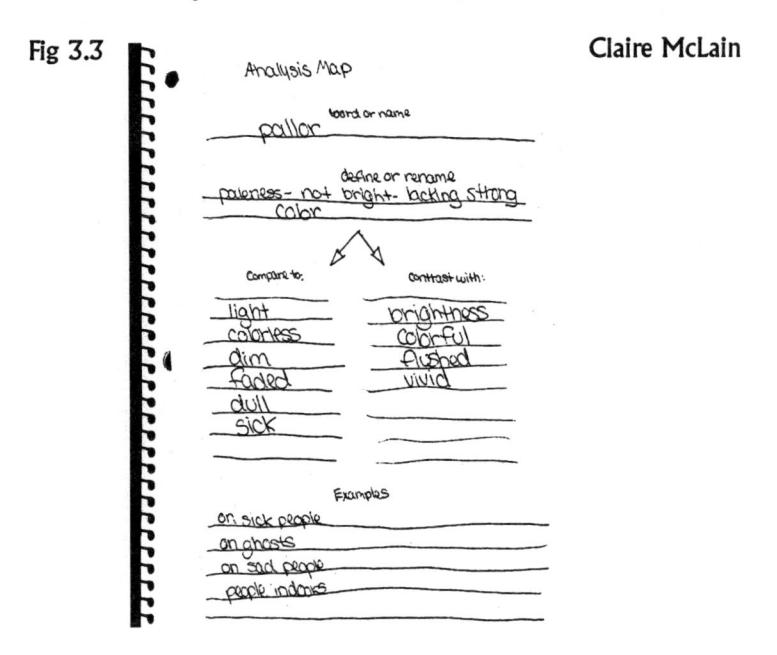

Fig 3.3   Claire McLain

Analysis Map

word or name: pallor

define or rename: paleness— not bright— lacking strong color

Compare to: light, colorless, dim, faded, dull, sick

Contrast with: brightness, colorful, flushed, vivid

Examples: on sick people, on ghosts, on sad people, people indoors

Fig 3.4   E.13 Linear Arrays
Sarah Mariott

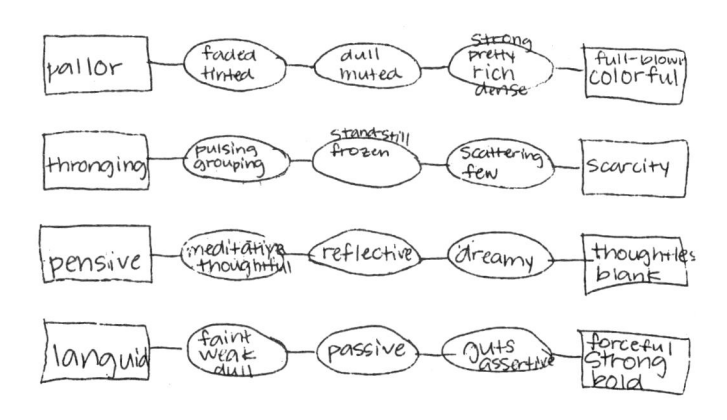

[pallor] — (faded, tinted) — (dull, muted) — (strong, pretty, rich, dense) — [full-blown colorful]

[thronging] — (pulsing, grouping) — (stand-still, frozen) — (scattering, few) — [scarcity]

[pensive] — (meditative, thoughtful) — (reflective) — (dreamy) — [thoughtless, blank]

[languid] — (faint, weak, dull) — (passive) — (juts, assertive) — [forceful, strong, bold]

Fig 3.5   Billy Pospisil

1st nine weeks
Context: drooping, weak — He had a longing, languid face as he watched his girlfriend leave him.

Word: Languid

Definition: droopy, weak
Possibilities: Heartbreaking
From context: being dumped, cheating

Common definition: Sad; Falling

Specialized Examples:
- Pansee jammy
- Bassett hounds face
- When you sad

personal experience
my dog's face

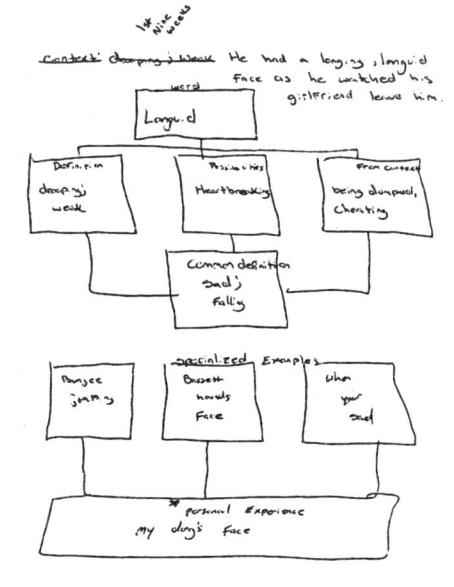

I take students through sixteen or seventeen different graphic organizers because each

Paula Brock   47   Nudges

uses a different activity and involves students in different kinds of tasks with the words they are studying. These different activities form a bank into which students deposit and from which they withdraw meanings to help them think about the words they are learning.

Students develop favorite organizers, ones that make sense to them and give them the clearest understanding of their words. They undoubtedly also choose organizers which seem the easiest. Perfect. If the activity seems easy to them, they will do it.

Evaluation

During the third week of our vocabulary study each grading period, students choose a partner and test each other over the five vocabulary words they have grabbed for dedicated study. Student A calls out Student B's words; Student B writes down the word and either its definition, or its synonym and antonym, or the original sentence in which it occurred. The vocabulary word does have to be spelled correctly, but any one of the three definitional choices constitutes a correct answer. Student A then grades Student B's paper. (In a five-word test, each number has two parts; so the correct spelling of the vocabulary word will count ten points, and any one of the three correct choices for definitions will count ten points.) Student B then reverses the process and tests and grades Student A's vocabulary words. Taking turns works best for me and my students; trying to test and grade simultaneously results in confusion and wastes class time.

I count these small tests as daily grades. I usually only have to modify this system for students who have identified perceptual limitations. When I record the grades for these students, I attach a tiny Post-It Note®, modify the grade, and write a note of encouragement about the small improvements that are always evident. (Make sure these students are paired with a friend, a sweet and sensitive partner, or another student who also struggles and wrestles with vocabulary study and will be likely to understand the other's Herculean efforts.)

When the first test is completed and graded, Student A and Student B go back to their individual VBCs and grab five new words to put on VGCs for study during week four. During the fifth week, Student A tests Student B on the five new words plus the first five words from week two; thereafter, the cycle repeats itself every two weeks. I am teaching under nine week grading periods; you would simply adjust this time table if your grading periods were different. Week seven tests the words from weeks three, five, and seven. Week nine tests the words from weeks three, five, seven, and nine; this last test I count as a major test grade.

The pulling out and studying of words is shaped like a layer cake in this system with most layers repeated at least once. At the end of the grading period, students have handled twenty new words. These words have been studied repeatedly, the sentences they originated from have been read and re-read, the words have come from meaningful contexts, and the chances of the words being remembered are vastly improved.

Grades may be taken at any or all of several places throughout this process, but VGCs strength lies in the highly individualized nature of the project. Conversely, in any entirely textbook-given or teacher-given vocabulary list, some students will know some of the words, some students will know most of the words, and some students will know none of the words. With VGC students study words they themselves identify as important to learn. My job is to model, monitor, encourage, and applaud.

Guiding Principles

A serendipitous advantage of VGC is also teaching the study strategy of spending little brain-friendly sips of time each day merely reading about words instead of unproductive marathon study sessions on teacher-given vocabulary lists. I know students still cram before the tests, but at least they do that for most words more than one time in this process; furthermore, I have directly taught them a productive study model. Some students recognize its value and use it right away, whereas some students remember it in the future and put it to work then.

Making It Easy

Many of the newly published literature textbooks support the idea that each student has to make his or her own way in the area of vocabulary improvement. These new books go a long way forward in helping students because they preview new vocabulary for students, show actual examples of how context clues work for new words, and provide on-the-spot definitions for many of the high-quality, substantive words students need to pull out of their reading and study. These texts give students a head start on the personal effort they must expend to grow their own vocabularies.

VBCs, VGCs, and VAP are labor intensive, requiring a high level of determination and dedication. It may seem that they require an inordinate amount of time, but the repetition and manipulation of these words mimics what reading widely produces in vocabulary growth. If students discipline themselves to read their VGCs everyday as a means of study, then they are reading and rereading wonderful sentences written by gifted and talented writers who use words correctly, aptly and artistically—a benefit to establishing a pattern or a pathway in the brain for these new words.

The Signs of Progress

Students become more adept at pulling important and useful vocabulary words out of their reading instead of just odd words. It is amazing how many VGC words appear on SAT words lists or would have been chosen were I still laboring to produce teacher-made vocabulary lists. Most importantly, students perceive VGC as fun and easy; they enjoy working together in pairs on the tests, and they learn from each other in the bargain. Students begin to feel more confident and successful when they see what they consider to be easy daily vocabulary grades accumulate in my gradebook.

As their vocabulary rings grow throughout the year, students are proud of the work they have done. Students leave my class with a personal dictionary of eighty vocabulary words they have studied, and many, many VBC words. They carry in their hands a visible record of hard work and perseverance. They know what they have learned and how they went about learning it – true metacognition.

Making It Easy

I don't want vocabulary study to seem like a steady diet of worksheets or dull seatwork, so I also ask:

- Students to find some of their words somewhere else. Students must provide proof of this somehow—a note from the librarian or a parent, a movie or play ticket, or a newspaper or magazine clipping, a photocopied page, or any other method of accountability we devise. Then I initial the source.
- Students to extend or integrate some of their words by:
    a. Displaying the multiple meanings of a word through a web, wheel, or some device they create;
    b. Differentiating a word from similar ones like homophones or frequently confused words;
    c. Using the word in their WN;
    d. Displaying a sentence that correctly uses the word.
- Students to play with their words by:
    a. Illustrating them or making cartoons with them;
    b. Dividing them into word parts or researching their etymology;
    c. Writing a four line (or more) poem that rhymes their word to others;
    d. Playing *Scrabble* or other word games where the players document the words each person makes;
    e. Having a vocabulary bee where I hold the students' twenty word vocabulary tests and have two teams compete for a small prize;
    f. Making a small crossword puzzle with several of their words.

Establishing the Reading/Writing Connection

There are wonderful picture books available to spark interest in vocabulary, have some fun with words, and change the pace. I use *The Weighty Word Book, Antics, There's an Ant in Anthony, The King Who Rained,* or *The Sixteen Hand Horse*. Such books may present words the students may not know.

Evaluation

With a system in place to grade the collection process (VBC) and the words pulled out for dedicated study (VGC), how will I grade the VAP? It is unrealistic to attempt to keep my hands and eyes on every element of this *volume* of vocabulary work. I want the students to care about what they are doing and how they are doing at it. If they have to assess themselves, they are more likely to attend to the work. A student may receive a paper I have graded and mutter, "She GAVE me a C!" But if that student grades his or her own paper, the outcome is much more likely to be tied to the realities of their own study and attention. It can't be as easily dismissed as the whims of a teacher, a teacher who doesn't like them, or a teacher having a bad day.

Guiding Principles

Do students cheat when they grade their own papers? I'm sure they do at times. But there are dozens of ways to cheat on worksheets, objective tests, reading assignments and other things in school. I believe cheating is its own reward; I also believe that I will not catch cheaters every time no matter how vigilant I am. I do talk to students about not cheating and not getting hard inside by cheating so that their conscience doesn't work as well anymore. Guilt trip? Maybe. I prefer to think that sometimes we all need to speak out clearly about what the abstract ideas of honor and truthfulness are about in practice. Since I have time to be up and around the room cheerleading their efforts, smoothing out difficulties, answering questions, suggesting options, and approving new ideas throughout this process, students tend to stay engaged and resist the temptation to cheat.

I return again and again to Monty Roberts's philosophy which is, "rooted in respect and ends with expectations clearly defined: People must be allowed to fail . . . but do not protect the lazy or incompetent; above all, people must be allowed to succeed and be rewarded if they meet or exceed the terms of the contract" (Roberts 244).

Evaluation

The grading rubric I use for the manipulation part of our vocabulary work works like this:

Twenty words multiplied by 3 points each = base grade:_____ (student computes this grade but gives me a visual check that all twenty pages are completed). Then the students write reflections for me about their vocabulary activities each term:

- what their favorite words were and why for 10 points
- what words they disliked and why for 10 points
- what words surprised them in some way for 10 points

For an additional 10 points, they write a separate sentence for each of three of their words that shows they know how to use that word correctly.

These student reflections total forty points, which I record as grades. I add my numbers to that total and arrive at a grand total that is recorded in my grade book.

The Importance of the Model

It seems important, given the trends for students to know more sooner than ever before, that something systematic be done to help students kindle a spark of enthusiasm for learning new words. Likewise, if the brain looks for patterns and connections, it seems prudent to try to fit vocabulary study into language arts activities in that way. This system for vocabulary study was born out of the way I work on words myself—noting them in the text, looking up the actual meanings, and then going back to the text to read again with deeper understanding.

Horse Sense

We spend our lives making meaning, learning the languages of our families, our pets, and our earth. To live richly, we should consciously attend to each vocabulary. It's easy, for instance, if a horse's ears are pinned and teeth bared, to tell he is prepared to do battle or bluff you into thinking he will. Harder to comprehend are the stillnesses, the flicking ears, the crowding of his body into your space that indicate a horse's aggravation and tendency to do something untoward momentarily.

Guiding Principles

When I layer over all that is physical and visual in communication the abstraction of language, there is also auditory, cerebral, and symbolic meaning. Vocabulary is the music and beat, the tone and the tempo of humans' symbolic system of communication, our language. I must use every possible means to provide students the ability to sing along.

WORKS CITED

Allen, Janet. *Words, Words, Words.* York, Maine: Stenhouse Publishers, 1999.

Gwynne, Fred. *The Sixteen Hand Horse.* New York: Simon and Schuster Inc., 1980.

_____ *The King Who Rained.* New York: Aladdin Paperbacks, 1970.

Hepworth, Cathi. *Antics.* New York: Putnam & Groset Group, 1992.

Levitt, Paul M., Douglas A. Burger, and Elissa S. Guralnick. *The Weighty Word Book.* Boulder, Colorado: Manuscripts, Ltd., 1985.

Most, Bernard. *There's An Ant in Anthony.* New York: Mulberry Books, 1980.

Roberts, Monty. *The Man Who Listens to Horses.* New York: Random House, 1996.

The Fourth Nudge

THE FOURTH NUDGE: SPELLING

The Story

Probably no other area of language arts is more maligned than spelling. Probably no other area in the purview of language arts is the path toward becoming a competent speller less understood. Probably no other skill is more obvious when lacking than spelling acumen. Probably no other marker is so widely applied to judge a person educated than whether he or she can spell conventionally. Probably no other desire is expressed more often by parents than the wish that I could teach their children to spell better.

I spent many years as a teacher expecting spelling to be taught and mastered in elementary school—well before they got to me in the ninth grade, thank you very much. Then I learned a little about the developmental nature of spelling and spent a couple of years just shrugging and proclaiming, "Well, spelling competency is developmental, you know; these kids will get it someday!"

Three years ago it dawned on me if students were poor spellers when they arrived at my classroom door, it was not all right to look backward and blame lack of knowledge on what I incorrectly guessed was ineffective instruction, nor was it all right to wish those same students luck in the future and hope they developed into passable spellers someday, somehow. Something had to be done, and guess who needed to figure out what that something was?

There are no spelling programs, textbooks, or ready-made spelling curricula, as far as I know, available for older students. Furthermore, with the mobility of society these days, students may come to my school with years of systematic spelling instruction behind them; cursory, hit-or-miss instruction; or absolutely no formal spelling instruction at all. Students come to my class as both excellent and abominable spellers, and every gradation in between.

The first thing I needed to do as a teacher was to learn something about spelling. I approached this task with trepidation because I wasn't sure I could learn the spelling language my elementary teacher friends could reel off, spouting words like *fricatives*, *dipthongs*, and *blends*. I also doubted my ability to learn now what I had failed to learn all those years I poured through spelling textbooks as a child. I was, after all, a good student with a record of high achievement, an avid reader, a journeyman writer, and a darn good speller. How come I did not already possess the body of rules and exceptions—the technical information that I so needed to impart to my students?

The Underpinnings

The mystery became unlocked when I read *SPEL is a Four Letter Word* by Richard

Gentry, *You Kan Red This* by Sandra Wilde, and "Developmental Writing and Spelling" in *Acts of Teaching* by Carroll and Wilson. These readings helped me understand the complexity and the teachability of spelling. Resource after reference emphasized the same principles:

- The need to distinguish between vocabulary acquisition and high-frequency spelling words;
- The need for a spelling study strategy that made much of the visual nature of spelling;
- Direct teaching of the four spelling rules that functioned reliably enough to be taught and learned.

This minimal research gave me a vision of where I was going as I planned spelling lessons for my students, but where would I get the spelling words for students to work on?

I came up with the brilliantly misguided idea to ask my students to list their own personal spelling demons. That was, as they say, an exercise in futility. Few students could conjure up any words they had difficulty spelling. Now I realize that when you put students on the spot, they often momentarily freeze and can't think of things to contribute. I also know that my students' inability to make a list out of the blue indicated the brain needed more priming. Sadly, the blank stares I encountered that day indicated that students were not directed towards thinking about their own learning; they were not actively cognizant of what they had learned, what they still needed to know, or how they might go about learning new things. So there I was still stuck in neutral wondering what spelling words were appropriate and needed for my students' progress as literate beings.

Fortuitously, our district adopted the Rebecca Sitton spelling program, and I was sent copies of the last active grade level of these books that offered direct spelling instruction. From those books I was able to get a list of the high frequency spelling words that students should know how to spell, grades one through eight. I have since found several such lists, so they are widely available.

The Strategy

From the research I had done, I decided upon four ways to begin to uncover the high frequency spelling words that each of my students did not know:

1. I wrote a short piece composed of as many high frequency spelling words from the Sitton list as I could put together in a meaningful way. I dictated this piece out loud to students, they wrote it word-for-word, and

then they highlighted any of the high frequency words they misspelled.
2. I gave students a mastery spelling test from the grammar and writing textbook used in my school. Again, students highlighted any of the words they misspelled from this activity.
3. I used activities for each of the four reliable spelling rules from Sandra Wilde's book, *You Kan Red This*, to generate words students could not automatically spell.
4. I marked high frequency words that students were misspelling in their writing and asked them to add these words to their spelling lists.

Diagnostic Strategy I: Dictation

The piece I wrote for dictation was an essay about becoming a ninth grader; it used as many of the seventh and eighth grade high frequency spelling words as I could possibly incorporate into it. (See Fig. 4.1) When students finished this dictation, I put a copy of it on the overhead with the high frequency words underlined. Students highlighted any words they missed, and printed them clearly and correctly in the left-hand margins of their dictation papers. I walked around the room and double-checked to make sure students copied the words down correctly from the overhead. I found some students looked at a key and then wrote the word down the same way they misspelled it in the first place; so with spelling, teachers need to check, double check, and check again. This activity usually gave students three or more words with which to begin their own personal spelling list.

Fig 4.1

SPELLING DICTATION

<u>Yesterday</u> I didn't have a <u>concern</u> in the world. My <u>identity</u> was <u>established</u> as a <u>leader</u>; I was the "top dog" of the Junior High <u>evolutionary</u> ladder - - I was an <u>eighth</u> grader. It was <u>perfect</u> because I was <u>popular</u>, <u>knew</u> what was required, was <u>excited</u> about the future, had a great group of **friends**, and was settled in the **routines** of my life.

Then life <u>threw</u> me a curve. I <u>arrived</u> at a pre-<u>arranged</u> <u>destination</u> called high school. I had <u>risen</u> to a new <u>height</u>, only to find myself at an all-time low. From the **principal** to the <u>cafeteria</u> <u>employee</u>, someone seems always <u>available</u> to <u>observe</u> my every action, <u>improve</u> my attitude, <u>convince</u> me <u>they're</u> right, <u>separate</u> me from my **friends**, and <u>prevent</u> me from doing what I want to do. This is a <u>serious</u> problem. To make things <u>worse</u>, my <u>parents</u> don't seem to <u>recognize</u> me anymore. They take every <u>opportunity</u> to check my <u>progress</u>, <u>review</u> every <u>angle</u>, <u>discuss</u> <u>personal</u> topics and <u>suggest</u> the best ways to **prepare** myself for everything!

But wait! <u>There's</u> a silver <u>lining</u>! With each passing day, I inch closer and closer to that <u>excellent</u> <u>condition</u>: the day I get my <u>driver's</u> <u>license.</u>

Diagnostic Strategy II: Grade Level Spelling Mastery Test

The textbook "Mastery" spelling test also included words from the Sitton high frequency list, words I expected my students to spell correctly. Students worked on the test, a key went up on the overhead, they highlighted the ones they missed, and then printed the words correctly in the margins of their papers. I checked their corrections to make sure the students had spelled them correctly.

Diagnostic Strategy III: Minilessons

The third diagnostic activity I used was activities for each of the four spelling rules that work reliably enough to be taught from *You Kan Red This* by Sandra Wilde. This book is an absolute treasure. Not only is it thorough and sound pedagogically in the light of current research, but Wilde has designed and included minilessons and activities. This is help at its finest. I decided to focus on one spelling rule every nine weeks' grading period. (We have four such grading periods, so working out the math wasn't too difficult for me.)

I started with the "i" before "e" rule. When I asked students and adults in summer workshops to list all the spelling rules they remembered, they always say *i* before *e* except after *c*. Often that is the only rule they remember, which proves the point. If spelling could be mastered by memorizing a set of rules, those of us who have had formal spelling instruction would be excellent spellers and we would remember all the rules and the jargon of sounds and symbols. The reverse is also interesting to contemplate: isn't it interesting that one of the rules that does work consistently enough to be taught is this *i* before *e* rule? (Do any of you, like me, upon writing a word in which this rule applies, find your mind *automatically* chanting, *i* before *e* except after *c*, or when sounded like *a* as in *neighbor* or *weigh*?)

Students listen to the *i* before *e* minilesson, copy the rule in their spelling spiral, and then do an activity page applying the rule. The key goes on the overhead, and the corrections are printed carefully beside each misspelled word.

Do Something Fun

My students have a single-subject spiral notebook for their spelling and vocabulary work, so we have been doing all of this diagnostic work in the pages of this spiral. I ask students to open the front of the spiral, decorate the inside front cover with the word *Vocabulary* (and whatever else they would like); then we turn the spiral over and upside down and decorate the inside back cover with the word *Spelling* (and whatever else they would like). Then we do vocabulary work from the front to the back as normal, but we do spelling from the back to the front and upside down for a little something different. Organizing the work in this way attaches an importance to it. We have a special book for these activities that acts as a textbook. Organizing the work this way makes sure that students can keep up with their spelling and vocabulary lists. Organizing the work this way is just wacky. I hope students' brains giggle when they turn their spirals upside down and work backwards.

We study three other spelling rules as the year goes by: doubling the final consonant, changing *y* to *i* before adding a suffix, and dropping or keeping the final *e*. Each of the activities associated with each rule give students anywhere from just a few spelling words to quite a few spelling words to work on. In addition, the nature and content of the activities themselves focuses upon commonly known spelling problem areas.

Diagnostic Strategy IV: Pull Spelling Words from Writing

To tailor my spelling efforts more exactly and specifically to each individual child, the last and continuous way to find high frequency spelling words that students need to learn how to spell is to call attention to the words they are misspelling in their own writing.

I cut 1" x 2" Post-It-Notes® into three pieces lengthwise, cutting down the 2" side. That leaves a small strip with some stick-um on it, and the small strip is still big enough for most spelling words. The page marker sized Post-It-Strips (1" x 3") might work better for some students because they are larger, but the volume of work my students do makes cutting the smaller strips more economical for me.

Explaining first what I will do and why, I stick up to three Post-It-Note® flags on student papers that come to me, either as finished products or as drafts brought to conferences. I place these flags in the margins of sentences where a high frequency word is misspelled; this way I signal the students, but they are given the responsibility and the ownership of finding the words themselves and correcting them. Be ready to help some students. There will always be some who cannot seem to locate the errors in their own papers. They become better proofreaders after they have to engage in this activity a few times.

Making It Easy

There may be many more misspelled words in any given draft, but if I want students to be willing to work on spelling, I can't drown them in a sea of sticky note flags that cry out, "Wrong, wrong, wrong!" before they get a chance to practice, review, or learn something about spelling. Since I do not take off points in the very beginning for misspelled words, students have no reason to see this flagging as anything other than a help or aid to them on their way to becoming more confident and competent spellers.

Developing the Strategy

I ask students to print every word they have misspelled from any of the four types of diagnostic activities onto one of the tiny Post-It-Note® strips. Then I check every one of every students' strips because I know that copying errors occur from the overhead to the desk. It certainly will not do students any good to write and study words that are spelled incorrectly, so I walk around and check and double-check. (Keep a dictionary in your hand for this—after you see words misspelled so many times in so many ways, all of a sudden you can't tell whether it's spelled correctly or not, yourself.)

Then, students turn to the spelling part of their spiral, and place their sticky notes down the left-hand side of the page. Moving horizontally across the page to the right, they write the words in a column in cursive, move further right and print the words in a column. The page looks like this:

(sticky note)	(written word)	(printed word)
separate	*separate*	separate
friend	*friend*	friend
license	*license*	license

(See Fig. 4.2)

    I teach students to deliberately form each letter as they print and write their spelling words. I have them take this step, although it's repetitive, because I want them to practice writing these high frequency words correctly. I also want a hard copy of their words on paper in case the Post-It-Note® strips lose their sticky and come off the page. It's a good idea to save four or five pages of the spelling spiral for these lists because we add to our personal spelling lists all year long.

Fig 4.2   Toni Rhoades

recognize	recognize	recognize
separate	separate	separate
principal	principal	principal
eighth	eighth	eighth
personal	personal	personal
they're	they're	they're
cafeteria	cafeteria	cafeteria
immediately	immediately	immediately
occurring	occurring	occurring
deceive	deceive	deceive
separate	separate	separate
pianos	pianos	pianos

Putting Ideas to Work

    I ask students to choose five of these identified spelling words, put them on a clean page of their spiral, put a box around them, and label them *1*. This is a good time to walk around the room and check the spelling of these boxed words yet another time. It does not take long, and it is absolutely imperative that students study words that are spelled correctly to begin with. I highlight each box as I check it, both as a signal to the student that these words are correct and eligible for study; highlighting also helps me keep up with where I am, which students I still need to see, which students have been absent, and clearly identifies any students who are not participating.

Important Instruction: A Spelling Study Strategy

The next thing I teach is a spelling study strategy. Almost any professional textbook for teaching spelling includes a spelling study strategy where students progress through steps such as these: writing the word, spelling the word out loud by pointing at each letter, closing their eyes in order to visualize the word, writing the word from that visual memory, and proofreading the written word letter-by-letter. As I go through the steps with a model word, I ask students to offer reasons why each step is done and why each step is in the order in which it is given.

When we get to the idea of spelling the word out loud and pointing to every letter, for instance, I give the example of the word *separate*. If *separate* is misspelled, it is usually misspelled by just one, single letter, for example: *sepErate*. I also teach my students about magic headphones. They put their elbows on the table, prop their chins on their thumbs, extend the fingers to cover the flap on the ears at the opening of the ear canal, and speak softly to themselves. This creates an echo chamber so when they speak the word, its letters reverberate in the head. Further, the strategy of magic headphones is so discreet no one needs to know that students care talking to themselves and wonder if they're off their rocker.

When we get to the idea of visualization, we talk about the power of seeing yourself hit the baseball, run the race successfully, or do well in a speech. Many people consider this mental practice as powerful as the physical exercise we do to achieve skill in various other areas of our lives.

Connecting Work to Life

I think this spelling study strategy is one of the most eloquent, graceful, valuable gifts I give my students all year long. It can be used and adapted for anything that needs to be committed to memory; it is simple, multi-sensory and quick. For students who have trouble focusing or have few, if any, study habits, this easy strategy gives them some structure, some definite steps, to follow.

Evaluation

I give students three weeks to study these five words. That may seem like an incredibly long time to study a teeny-tiny number of words, but keep in mind what I am trying to do. I want things to seem easy to my students. Many spelling experts point out that twenty spelling words per week is a ridiculously high expectation, so

I would rather err on the side of the students as far as the amount of work is concerned. These are high frequency words, words they know and use. But something has happened as academics have moved forward so fast to some students. Many seem lost, left behind in the dust of scope and sequence. Maybe they didn't really have time to get the lessons the first time, maybe the lessons were inappropriate or unclear, maybe the student was stressed, distracted, or simply disinterested. Whatever the reason, the reality is that the students we teachers grieve over, wonder about, and try to rebound are those who seem injured by educational systems. They are shut down or out, sometimes, by repeated educational failure. It is also more and more obvious to me that the regular 'ole Jack and Jill students, the ones who appear to be doing fine getting all their credits, are not enjoying school, or often feel like captives. So why not make it seem easy for them?

Horse Sense
When training a young horse and advancing him up to the next level, sometimes he gets confused. He may dance all around or balk and refuse to try anymore. If he gets entirely frustrated, he will try to escape what he sees as punishment anyway he can; and believe me, he has quite a strength and size advantage with which to summarily dismiss your attempts to push him forward through the lesson. How much better to just stop and go back to kindergarten school, the first baby steps, go back to what he already knows. Do some easy things, restore his confidence, his peace, and he will try again to advance to the next level. Keep hammering him and his escapes will become more pronounced and more violent.

Think what an additional vise schools put kids in. Schools impose on students with their thinking brains the insidious idea that they shouldn't revolt against that which confuses or frustrates them. The horse at least doesn't have to worry about being bad. He just explodes and escapes and snorts nervously, happy that he lived through the ordeal. As a teacher I want to avoid all that. Go back and do some easy stuff, calm the spirit and open the minds back up. Much better.

Do Something Fun
Just like everything else I do in the classroom, with spelling I move back and forth regularly from the known to the unknown; and, I find ways to manipulate what we are learning. Alphabet macaroni, plastic magnet letters, and Alphabits® cereal are fun ways to create spelling words. Letter beads and pipe cleaners can be used to make "spelling word of the month" bracelets. Alphabet letter stamps and stamp pads can be used to stamp the words into the spelling spirals, and onto student's hands, arms and hopefully their brains. Students are usually willing to buy Vis-à-vis® pens to write spelling words on bathroom mirrors at home.

The Underpinnings

Phonics They Use by Patricia Cunningham is a wonderful resource chock full of activities to use with high frequency spelling words. Some of these activities are loud, some are quiet, some use movement, some are silly; but the sheer variety of possibilities allows plenty of freshness to keep students engaged. Do something fun in the classroom every week that lets students practice their spelling words, and do not forget picture books. There are wonderful books that play with homophones and imbed little words within more sophisticated ones; and, many picture books directly teach phonics lessons that play the dual role of helping word attack skills and spelling. Strickland in *Teaching Phonics Today* says it this way, " . . . teachers using trade books as core materials are more likely to capitalize on the opportunities for phonics instruction presented in the literature rather than rely on a rigidly applied hierarchy of skills" (30).

The Importance of the Model

I also have each student make a *Portable Word Wall* on the inside of their colored classroom collection folder; they copy all of their personally diagnosed high frequency misspelled words in the proper alphabetical boxes on this folder. Again: I check every word that is written on each student's portable word wall. Time spent checking to begin with will prevent unnecessary errors later on! Every time students write, revise, or edit a paper, they use these spelling word walls. I cannot over-emphasize the importance of students of all ages having access to a Word Wall for high frequency spelling words. Word Walls are mentioned in almost every book that addresses spelling as an efficacious means of improving student spelling achievement. Students perform better if I lay aside the old lock-step, linear instructional methods as well as my prejudices that certain things are too primary or too advanced my teaching.

Evaluation

In my class, we take a spelling test every nine weeks. The first test covers only five words (I have been awfully busy diagnosing needs, you know.); the second covers the first five words plus five new ones; and the system pyramids like that throughout the year. Twenty words mastered in a whole year may not sound like much improvement, but if they know they can dependably spell those twenty, learn how to attack their remaining spelling demons, have only four rules to remember, have better skill at proof-reading, and know they have a much improved visual spell-check, of course they walk away from a year's spelling instruction feeling empowered.

Guiding Principles

Spelling is a dip stick for measuring fluency in language arts even though there "appears to be no rigid sequence of development that all children follow as they learn to spell" (Strickland 21). While I believe there will always be learners for whom correct spelling remains mysterious, just as I know I will probably always have to look up my nemesis patterns: *accommodate* and *commitment*—still much could and should be done to give students more skill and confidence as spellers. Lacking ability and fluency as spellers has to be a major cause of losing the desire to write and read. Literacy does not grow through practicing isolated skills; rather, literacy grows by binding many skills together so that they lead to meaning-making and understanding. I'm not expecting my students to become perfect spellers in one year; however, I am expecting them to gain the long-term skills to get themselves there eventually.

WORKS CITED

Carroll, Joyce Armstrong and Wilson, Edward. *Acts of Teaching.* Englewood, Colorado: Teacher Ideas Press, 1993.

Cunningham, Patricia. *Phonics They Use.* New York: HarperCollins, 1995.

Gentry, Richard. *Spel is a Four-Letter Word.* NH: Heinemann, 1987.

Sitton, Rebecca. *Spelling Sourcebook 4.* Spokane, WA: Egger Publishing, Inc., 1995.

Strickland, Dorothy S. *Teaching Phonics Today.* Newark, Delaware: International Reading Association, 1998.

Wilde, Sandra. *You Kan Red This!* Portsmouth, NH: Heinemann, 1992.

The Fifth Nudge

THE FIFTH NUDGE: POETRY

The Story

Determining what pieces of literature to introduce for whole-class study is not a hard thing to do. Usually much choosing is done long before we teachers come on board and begin teaching in a district; often the choosing is determined by which literature book is adopted; sometimes the choosing is determined by a majority vote of teacher representatives sitting on curriculum committees.

The hard thing to do, is to *not* fall into the trap of letting a prescribed literature curriculum be what you do with students starting at the beginning of a textbook and marching through it one chunk of literature at a time. I was that teacher for many years, and my professional life seemed so simple. All I had to do was assign a poem, story, act of a play, or chapter of a novel; lecture to the students about what it all meant and how it impacted their lives; do a project or two; have a film or recording or related speaker; double-check that I met all the essential elements of teaching; have students answer some of the questions at the ends of the selections; test the selection objectively; and slide blithely through a year of instruction feeling great about maintaining order and pace and having only a few failures on the books. I wonder how many students knew for sure after a year with me that I was a nice person who was generous with them about late work, but they still just simply hated English class?

Winds of Change

When I began studying the writing process, and through it a return to learning and understanding the *significance* of cognitive developmental theory and the findings of brain research, I began to understand that that the teaching of literacy was not about programs or textbooks. Teaching language arts is about discovering the interstices of the various parts of this subject area and *deliberately integrating* these components into the experience of each individual student.

Thought of in this way, I can read Vygotsky, Bruner, Emig, Smith, Elbow, Graves, Zinzer, Allen, Carroll and Wilson, and the many other wonderful thinkers who have shaped my work, and still function with textbooks, administrators, and colleagues who eschew professional reading.

Further, I can truly offer students a new chance to become readers and writers, fully endowed members of the literacy club, empowered to understand and flourish in whatever environment may be theirs in the future. I can help students reconnect as learners, become aware of their own processes, and strengthen their desire to continue learning.

And last but certainly not least, I can taste the joys of *making sense* of reading, writing, and teaching myself—not just repetitive, rote, deadening, going-through-the-motions teaching for twenty or thirty years—but rather the intense satisfaction that comes from knowing I have provided the best quality instruction for every student that I possibly could. I become a learner again, a fellow sojourner, and part of the team.

Scaffolding
 I love to start with poetry as the area of literary study each new school year because using poetry allows me to open many doors of thought in rapid succession. Poetry forms the basis for unparalleled talk about reading and writing processes, skills, and possibilities. Poems are often short, and this appeals to our nano-second, immediate feedback, give-it-to-me-now culture. Teaching poetry allows me to suggest all the beauty and music of language that should be present in all other writing genres and is often characteristic of the books we choose to read ourselves.
 I love to place poetry first because immersing ourselves in poetry and finding out about poems metamorphosizes students. They groan at the mention of poetry because they've come to feel that poetry is too vague and obtuse to be understood, but it is by far the most popular part of our work together according to students' end-of-year written course reflections.

Making It Easy
 Poetry is the perfect nudge into participation in the classroom because it's easy to devise minilessons, group activities, and models that lend themselves to coaxing similar writings from students. Since many poems are short, the task does not seem so overwhelming and students figure at least the torture will not last too long.

The Importance of Models
 Poetry is simply the perfect scaffold for reading and writing as much as anything because studying and writing poetry allows us to begin building a safe, accepting, literary climate in the classroom. Every poem written, no matter its rhyme or lack of it, can be praised; *something* literary can be pulled out of it to talk about, even if it is as simple as showing how to change the first letter(s) of words to create word families. If we start listing word families on the boards during class time, we undoubtedly uncover vocabulary words that some students in the classroom do not know; and we undoubtedly uncover some sound-alike words that are spelled differently, often misspelled, or sometimes confused.

Fostering Further Thinking
 In this way, we make the point again and again that we must monitor our mean-

ing when we write. We also create a happy collage of colorful words to be used as a bank. I get active participation from more students than had I handed them a worksheet. Most importantly, they have fun doing something that seems easy, while I have activated the thinking of everyone present (at least a better percentage than when I taught traditionally).

Do Something Fun

Many students who declare they cannot write poetry begin by writing what might kindly be called silly little jingles. Imagine their surprise, and rising estimation of themselves, when they learn what a rhyming couplet is, or when they read a poem like "Next" by Ogden Nash. Suddenly end rhyme, internal rhyme, near rhyme, and rhyme scheme have purpose and make sense to students. Further, it is a short step for students from writing those silly little jingles that make us laugh to purposeful couplets that maintain and sophisticate that humor. Adolescents may be silly and immature on purpose or accidentally in poetry and still save face.

Connecting Old Knowledge to New

Bringing poetry into the classroom is painless for me, too; the main responsibilities I have for teaching poetry are a firm foundation in the poetic elements, the terminology for talking about poems, and a willingness to approach poetry openly and with enthusiasm. Textbooks are rich with interpretation, poetic device explanation, and multiple connections; textbooks can ground me, as teacher, and give me a starting point or a base to spring from in working with students on poems. Poetry trade books abound that fill out my teaching repertoire and give countless ideas for concrete, creative things to do to help breathe life into poetry study for students. Study poetry. Re-approaching it myself in the same way I teach students to approach it, I become as a learner ready to taste and enjoy and ponder and discuss.

Ideas Behind the Ideas

Poems are fun for classroom study because all a poem needs to be successful with students is the passion of the one presenting it; and, if I am not a master of the theatre arts, there are always poems on tape and poems on video. Poems may be put on overhead transparencies, presented through computer programs, and displayed on posters. Varied kinds of sensory modes of presentation make the experience of a poem fresh and memorable for students. Poems may be tasted, seen, heard, smelled and touched if the presentation is designed for those effects. Poems may be read individually or with from two-to-many voices all at once. Poems may be interactive. The possibilities are endless and easy to do in class. All of a sudden, I look up and students are meeting poems everywhere—poems are being heard, felt, seen, and dreamed. Poems are, literally, in the air.

The Underpinnings

Once the stage is set, and poetry is flowing in our classroom, I make my teacher move. Poetry is the perfect genre to teach students about the purpose of language and to bring students back to the overarching theme of my work with them: Writing is the making of meaning and reading is the retrieval of meaning. When we study poetry, we do not simply go through the motions by learning a few terms, a genre, or a body of literature. We use poetry to find out how to express ourselves more aptly and richly. We use poetry to find out how to read more comprehensively and deeply. As long as students hold on to the idea that poems mean whatever I, the teacher, wants them to mean, then they can be present but not really work as a reader or a thinker because they staunchly maintain they either like or don't like poetry. My job, then, becomes nudging them to see broad, general, useful, and "for always" things from studying poetry.

Most poems employ just a few poetic devices, so technically they are not beyond us. Because poems differ in style, tone, topic, type, length, and tempo, we don't get tired or bored. The compact nature of poetry allows us to invoke Rosenblatt's transactional notion of reading (Rosenblatt —) and look at poems from the three perspectives of what the words literally say, what the poet probably meant, and what personal connections/meanings we each may make with the poem without getting lost in a deep, intensive reading activity. In short, poetry shows students where skill, art, and meaning meet.

Learning Poetic Terminology

What I have students do with poetry is ridiculously easy. First, I give them a V. I. P. gold paper clip to mark off five pages (fronts and backs) in their WN; they label this section, "Poetry Sampler" (see figure 5.1).

Fig 5.1   Claire McLain

Poetry Sampler

<u>Metaphor</u> - the comparison of two essentially unlike things pg. 1004, 799

<u>Couplet</u> - two rhyming lines of poetry ex pg 36

<u>rhyme scheme</u> pattern of rhyming in a poem.

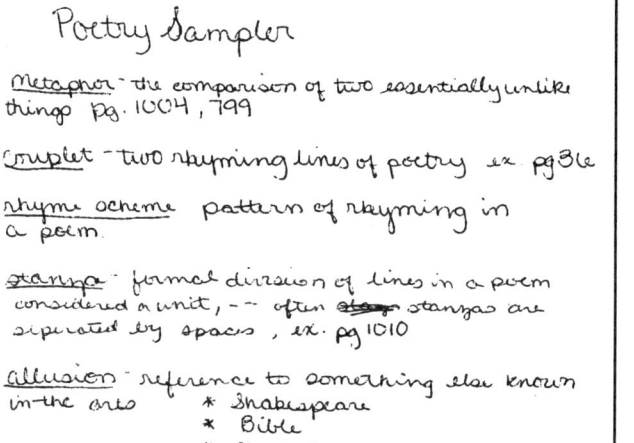

<u>stanza</u> - formal division of lines in a poem considered a unit, -- often stanzas are separated by spaces, ex. pg 1010

<u>Allusion</u> - reference to something else known in the arts
  * Shakespeare
  * Bible
  * Mythology

<u>Repetition</u> - The repeating of words/phrases/chorus' in a poem

<u>Alliteration</u> - Repetition of consonant sounds

<u>Parallelism</u> - similar structure & similar meaning
    or "   "   + opposite meaning

Every time I teach a poetic device or poetic term, we write it down in this section, define it, and write an example or two from the poems we are studying. Normally, we cover the following:

Personification	Rhyme scheme	Onomatopoeia	Repetition
Metaphor	Internal rhyme	Alliteration	Inverted order
Simile	End rhyme	Assonance	Shifts
Symbolism	Slant rhyme	Allusion	Diction
Imperfect rhyme	Free verse	Parallelism	Narrative Poetry
Lyric	Sonnet (two main types)		

If my scope and sequence omits certain poetic elements yours includes, simply add them. The list above is in no way comprehensive or exhaustive, but it does give my students some *basic* terminology and a *basic* language to use in discussing most poems. Students always want to add poetic license to this list. This suggestion is perfect because it allows me to teach that tossing away any literary conventions is *always done purposefully.* Then I dare them to write a poem where they suspend the rules on purpose in order to convey their poem's meaning more effectively. Remember the purpose of my work with students in their WN (chapter 3). I want to develop over a year's time a repository of tools, strategies, techniques, writing ideas and serendipitous discovery models that will be useful to students as they write. We put this Poetry Sampler, our knowledge of beautiful, musical language, in our WN.

Hands On Learning
Simultaneous to all the reading and oral discovery of poems, I also want to get poems on the fingertips of students. We do as many concrete, hands-on, group activities with poems as we can. For example:

1. Each student gets five different colored 3x5 index cards. They label each card with one of the five senses (i.e., the pink card would be labeled *sight*, the yellow card would be *hearing*, the green card would be *taste*, and so on). We go outside for five minutes of absolute silence where students record the things they can hear, see, smell, taste, or feel on the labeled cards. Back inside, students prioritize the cards they like best and put them on the board in sensory, color-coded groups. I make sure each color has at least three cards so that each sense is represented.

Pink	Green	Blue	Yellow	Lavender
____	____	____	____	____
____	____	____	____	____
____	____	____	____	____

Then I read the cards as a poem, saying, "It's August in Texas, I can see card #1, card #2, card #3; I can hear card #1, card #2, card #3;" and so on. I invite students to write their own sensory poem, using their own cards or any ideas they've gotten from the whole group poem. (Save this activity for a crisp, cold day or a rainy day – a day senses will be heightened.)
2. I read *Hailstones and Halibut Bones* by Mary O'Neill, *Color* by Ruth Heller, *A Song of Colors* by Judy Hindley, or better yet, read all three. Asking stu-

dents to pick a color to write a poem about, I always have the biggest box of Crayola crayons I can find available for this activity because it's fun for students to choose a unique or unusual color from the big box to write about. Students share their poem with one person at their table, and then they share with the whole table. Meanwhile, I circulate among the tables, looking for errors that might embarrass upon publication like correct word choice (there/their/they're) or spelling inconsistencies. Then students carefully copy their color poem on colored or white paper, writing with crayola, and spatter-painting them with diluted water color paints. We display the finished poems around the room.

3. Broken crayolas are shaved in hand-held pencil sharpeners. Students get two 5 x 7 pieces of waxed paper and a heaping tablespoon of crayola shavings. With supervision and a low temperature iron, students iron the shavings between the two pieces of waxed paper and are then invited to write a poem about the activity, about the materials, about ironing, about whatever connects the activity to students' thoughts. The waxed paper picture is mounted on an 8 1/2 x 11 card stock in which a window has been cut to reveal the waxed design. The poem's draft is checked as in the color poems (#2 above), and then recopied above, below, or around the waxed design. These poems are beautiful mounted on windows.

4. Putting students in groups of four, I have them decide upon a topic, and then have each contribute a line to a four-line stanza. Together they write a second stanza for their poem. They share orally with the whole class.

5. Each student writes a title and the first line of a poem. I ring a bell, everyone stands and scrambles to someone else's poem. Students sit, add a line to the poem of a classmate; and then I ring the bell for scrambling yet again. Scramble a minimum of four times; I usually have them scramble eight times. When students return to their own seats, they read "their" poem and then we share around. Initial ground rules need to be established for this activity. For instance, there should be no running or knocking anyone down to get to a chair; there should be no defacement or scribbling on anyone else's paper; and nothing inappropriate or mean-spirited may be written on someone else's poem.

6. I use books like *Just People–Paper, Pen and Poem* by Kathi Appelt and *Where I'm From, Where Poems Come From* by George Ella Lyon that have poems and then invitations for students to write in response.

7. We do lots and lots and lots of writing off the text. "It helped me to see that it is natural to take on someone else's style, that it is a prop that

you use for a while until you have to give it back. And it just might take you to the thing that is not on loan, the thing that is real and true: your own voice" (Lamott 195). Sharing poems from every resource I can gather, the kids to try to copy the style, rhythm, and rhyme of a line or two of the original. I always ask for volunteers to share their resulting poems.
8. Students brainstorm a list of human emotions or feelings. As a class they choose the eight most important or often seen emotions. Folding a piece of paper into eight sections, they label each section with one of the eight chosen emotions. *Using lines only* (no colors and no recognizable designs like hearts or stars), students draw a design for each emotion. Then students walk silently around the room looking at everyone else's drawings. When students return to their own seats, they may adjust their own drawings; then they try to write a poem for each of the eight emotions, or for a combination of emotions, or about emotions, or about how feelings look, or about how drawing releases emotion, or about whatever this activity has given them to write about.

These in-class poetry experiences have put poems at the students' fingertips, in their eyes and ears, in their thoughts. Remember, I want poems to literally vibrate in the air. I ask students to continue writing poems of their own. Variety, experimentation, play, and deliberation are the only required ingredients of this assignment.

Strategy: Variety and Experimentation
I ask students to write from different ideas, with different perspectives, with differing lengths, with a variety of poetic devices. I invite students to write from different voices, for a variety of purposes. I nudge students to avoid most patterns because many want to recycle the haiku poems they wrote in earlier grades. I also don't accept what I consider cheap efforts like acrostic poems made from their names or poems written from graphic organizers. All they have to do is try different things and flex their writing muscles.

Strategy: Play and Deliberation
While students play around writing poems with the variety I've invited, I want them to *recognize* what they are doing. At the bottom of each completed poem, they tell me what literary device(s) they put to work in that poem. After they've been writing for about four weeks, we spend some time sharing the best of the poems they have cooking by this time. Originated in the work of Peter Elbow, "Pointing" is described as a group sharing strategy in *Acts of Teaching* (Carroll and Wilson 151). Pointing has the structure necessary to allow groups of students to truly help each

other while at the same time applying a soft nudge. Pointing is easy to do and is kind to the writer who may be squirming under the discomfort of going public with writing that may all of a sudden not seem so good to him. Pointing simply invites listeners to point out what they like.

Revise and Reformulate
To begin the process of revision, I ask students to write sections from their drafts that include poetic devices. Student by student, we work together as a class thinking out loud about whether the devices are truly there or whether they are successfully employed. While this takes away some individual autonomy, it is important because it reinforces the understanding and deliberate use of poetic devices. Instead of just having poetic devices degenerate to merely something students have to memorize definitions for or identify in poetry test questions, suddenly these devices come alive for students and go to work for them to enhance and clarify what they want to express. Further, this work together allows peer review and editing help from me so that when the finished products do come to me for assessment, they will rate high marks, suitable to the effort the students have put into the process and indicative of what they have truly learned.

Introducing Conferencing
Besides the poems we published together in classroom activities, I ask students to share, revise, and polish five poems. As these poems are chosen, I introduce students to the concept of conferencing with others on their writing (most of my students seem to think that just sharing their work with someone is a conference). I spend time brainstorming and teaching the students what kinds of questions to ask of themselves, other writers, and their teacher in order to get the help or feedback they need. Further, as they think about what questions they need to ask, they are drawn into what they want the poem to say; they are eager to learn how to best get their message across.

Connecting Work to Life
At this point in the writing, grammar becomes an apparent need in the students' work, and the students themselves become teachable, ready to refine their meaning, word choice and punctuation. In addition, this is the place in the process that drives my instruction as well. In the students' poems I see the needed skills (like high frequency spelling words that are being misspelled and writing conventions that still need work). Also, I see the temperaments, tendencies, soft spots, and personalities of my students. It is imperative that I remember the students themselves and not just the subject matter that needs to be taught. Grammar and usage now become mean-

ingful to students and abstract rules start to make sense. Ratiocination (Carroll and Wilson 226-230) and Clocking (Carroll and Wilson 282-284) then become the crown jewels of revision and polishing, and students gain the confidence and skill as writers that they have often considered out of their reach.

Publication I

I find that I have to *require* at least one poem per student be submitted for formal, outside-of-school publication. Some wonderful poems have gone unpublished in the last few years due to a simple failure to follow through. Students nowadays are so stressed and short of time that even those who intend to submit their work for publication somehow just don't get it done. (And can't we all identify with the modern time squeeze?) Time has to be allotted in class, and students need to be guided through the submission process for poems to actually end up being sent out for publication.

Publication II

Meanwhile, we publish at least one poem in house. I ask students to pick one of their finished poems that would lend itself to illustration. They copy it on anything from a one-fourth to a full sheet of poster board, and illustrate the finished product in some way. The poem can be copied on the poster board in any fashion desired: handwritten, printed, calligraphied, using computer fonts or whatever; the only requirement is that if the poster is hung high on a wall, the print must be large enough to be readable from the floor.

The poem is illustrated in some way, and it is debatable whether students choose the poem they like best or choose the poem that lends itself most easily to illustration. Either way is perfectly acceptable. The illustrations may be done by the writer, a friend, or a relative. (When students are invested in their writing, they often want the art to do more justice to the writing than they themselves can produce; a guest artist is the perfect solution.) The illustrations may be any media and any format from color to collage, from stick figures to shapes to delicate watercolors. The finished product may be one dimensional or multi-dimensional. The art, or lack of it, in and of itself is not graded; rather, the poem is counted as one of the five poems required to fulfill the assignment and serves as a celebration of learning about, writing, and publishing poetry.

Horse Sense

I realize that using this approach to poetry sounds almost too good to be true. Go with me again to the horse pen and think about what makes a moving horse poetry in motion. A young horse may be awkward and tentative and unable to perform certain advanced movements under saddle; but watch him loose in the pasture where he is free to experiment and is not punished for failures, and we will see just how agile and stunning he can be. If I can give that horse the skills and tools to reproduce those movements under saddle and on cue while having those same conditions of freedom and support, I'll watch that horse grow into a confident, collected creature who truly glides across the ground.

Integration of Reading and Writing

Studying poetry allows me to center instruction on reading at the same time I am centering instruction on writing, fully integrating the two and showing students how reading illuminates writing and writing empowers reading. I match at least one poem deliberately to each of the eight strategies that have been identified that proficient readers use when they read:

- A poem that is easy *to connect to existing knowledge;*
- A poem that lends itself to *questions asked before, during, and after reading;*
- A poem that requires *inferencing;*
- A poem long enough to tax comprehension—where I can stop and start students and show them *how to monitor their comprehension;*
- Different poems on different days where I can show students how to employ *fix-up strategies* (like visualizing, rereading, retelling, predicting, and so forth) when meaning breaks down for them;
- Any poem can be used to *determine what's important in its content;*
- A poem that encourages *synthesis* to create new thinking (how has this poem helped you think in different ways?);
- Poems full of *sensory imagery* (Harvey and Goudvis 20-25).

I also use poetry to teach a minilesson for each of the three deep structures that readers use to comprehend text:

"*Semantic cues* . . . meaning(s), concepts, and associations of words and longer pieces of texts, including understanding subtle definitions and nuances.

Schematic cues . . . the reader's prior knowledge and/or personal experiences. They allow the reader to understand and remember what has been read. (These cues also group and organize new information in memory.)

Pragmatic cues . . . what the reader considers important and what he or she needs to understand for a particular purpose. They also include the social construction of meaning, in which groups of readers arrive at shared meaning and increasingly abstract interpretations (PEBC 2000)" (Tovani 18).

The Story

While the deep structures and proficient reader strategies are my primary focuses because they are so rarely deliberately taught, teaching poetry also allows me to huddle individually with students whose few word attack skills leave them unable to do more than wrestle with reading. While I've done some things all along in my work with students to support those who read below grade level, many do still need individualized instruction or reinforcement of the three surface structures that are "typically emphasized during the primary grades and provide the reader with visual and auditory clues for recognizing and pronouncing words as well as understanding sentence structure: graphophonic cues, lexical cues, and syntactic cues" (Tovani 18). If I give these students even a little one-on-one instruction it helps give them the courage they need to try to work so far above their reading skill level.

I have struggled to find the means, the lessons, and the concrete methods to be able to *teach* my students to both love and understand what they read. Obviously, isolated practice/worksheets on main idea, inference, plot, point-of-view, and theme do not work any better for teaching reading than isolated grammar practice does for teaching writing. Further, even by trying to cover reading skills with literature circles and vibrant class activities and discussions, I still had far too many apparently fluent readers—readers who could dance nimbly through text as they read aloud in class—but then confessed to me, "I can't tell you what I just read," or "I didn't understand a thing from what I just read," or "I don't remember a thing from what I just read."

Winds of Change

In the last two years a number of books have been published that address these issues of word callers: readers who can read but don't, and fake readers, readers who call words but don't comprehend (Tovani 2). What these books do is concentrate on the strategies that have been found to help readers; and, many of these books also provide the strategy lessons and discovery experiences that address the problems. Because of all the characteristics of poetry that I've already extolled - - its variety in subject, length, and purpose—and the sheer interest its language and poetic devices provide—poetry is the genre of choice to introduce reading strategies that work to put students back in an *active role* as readers. No strategy, idea, technique, minilesson, curriculum, or instruction is as important to students in learning to read as is the making sense from the reading (Smith 9).

I am still learning exactly what to do and what poems to use, and I especially have work to discover the best *order or sequence* to use as I unfold these strategies to students. Perhaps this will never be set in my mind because each new group of students brings their own unique knowledge base each year; however, what seems pivotal in every case is that the students must *engage* themselves in the process and think about what they are doing and whether it is working for them or not. Further, it is the vital that I address students' reading deficiencies.

The Underpinnings
Reading has become too automatic for these students; they read without thinking about it much. We have all probably had something like this happen to us: We get in the car to go somewhere and suddenly find ourselves there without really remembering anything at all about the trip. Such a ride scares the willies out of most reasonable people, but students have learned to tolerate this non-reading and need to be nudged back to active participation as readers. The proof of this in my own experience is that my students readily admit they read something they didn't understand or can't remember, but they don't seem troubled by this fact.

Another proof, of course, is that I've done exactly the same thing—begun reading something and suddenly discovered my mind was "some otherwhere" as Shakespeare described the love-struck Romeo. The difference is that I have the reading skills of long-practice to do something about the problem. Students will either read the passage over again; or, more likely, they will stop reading entirely, shrugging off their confusion and telling themselves it doesn't matter anyway because someone somewhere can explain the passage to them and they won't have to read it at all.

Guiding Principles
Reading is as necessary to me as breathing. I start the year with poetry because it reaches the heart faster than anything else and allows me to make connections with my students as soon as I can. I start the year with poetry because the genre possesses an uncanny compression of skills and beauty. I start the year with poetry because it is so easy for students to read and write, and nothing develops the desire to try better than seemingly painless success. I start the year with poetry because I love it, and I love what I have seen it do for my students in the past. The only way to start a fire with students is to be on fire myself.

WORKS CITED

Appelt, Kathi. *Just People & Paper/ Pen/ Poem*. Spring, Texas: Absey & Company, 1996.

Carroll, Joyce Armstrong and Wilson, Edward E. *Acts of Teaching*. Englewood, CO: Teacher Ideas Press, 1993.

Harvey, Stephanie and Goudvis, Anne. *Strategies That Work*. York, Maine: Stenhouse Publishers, 2000.

Heller, Ruth. *Color*. New York: Putnam & Grosset, 1995.

Hindley, Judy. *A Song of Colors*. Cambridge: Massachusetts, 1998.

Lamott, Anne. *Bird by Bird*. New York: Doubleday, 1994.

Lyon, George Ella. *Where I'm from, where poems come from*. Spring, Texas: Absey & Company, Inc., 1999.

O'Neill, Mary. *Hailstones and Halibut Bones*. New York: Doubleday, 1961.

Rosenblatt, Louise. *The Reader, the Text, the Poem*. Carbondale: Southern Illinois University Press, 1978.

Tovani, Cris. *I Read It, But I Don't Get It*. Portland, Maine: Stenhouse Publishers, 2000.

The Sixth Nudge

THE SIXTH NUDGE: FOSTERING ENGAGEMENT

The Story

None of the rest of this book means anything if I cannot make it possible for my students to foster and cultivate within themselves the discipline to cooperate with me and each other in a desire to learn, to engage in the lessons offered. None of the rest of this book is as complex as the reasons why disengagement or downright sabotage are the major difficulties I face every day as I enter school. "There is a constant struggle between the need to be an individual and the need to belong to a group. Both needs are natural and healthy, but the struggle between them is at the heart of much of the difficulty of organizational, family and social life. We want to be an individual, but we resist being isolated. Our relationship and commitment to work is a constantly moving tension between engagement and disengagement. Experiences either draw us in or push us away. They either create resistance, which results in fighting or fleeing, or they create commitment and collaboration" (Roberts xxx).

Why students do or do not bring as much of themselves to the educational experience as we wish they would is the pivotal issue upon which I lavish most of my energy as a teacher and upon which teachers are held, perhaps, even more responsible than they are for their subject matter. In my career I've seen concern fall on teacher training programs, teacher competency, career ladders, and the need for stricter teacher accountability. In a newspaper editorial recently, I discovered a blunt statement that the problem was the lack of teacher creativity. Major universities now are beginning to promote teacher as scholar programs, again seeming to aim at the idea that if teachers would just approach their jobs more intellectually and professionally, student inertia would come to an abrupt end.

Horse Sense

Years ago my daughter learned in Nancy Cahill's round pen how to get a young horse to step into a lope (canter or gallop) on the right lead (stepping off on the foot you asked them to by the cues you gave them). Sitting on the fence watching one day, I remarked to Nancy my wonder at how my daughter would stop the horse before he moved even one foot, set him back up, and ask for the lead again. I couldn't see that he'd even started, much less done anything wrong, and I couldn't understand the correction.

"You're looking at the wrong end of the horse," Nancy said, "You've got to look at the rear end to see that the horse is not gathering himself correctly so that he will be set up to take the correct lead."

Identifying the Problem

So looking at the teachers, or at *any one single cause* for the disengagement we see in modern students is looking at the wrong end of the horse.

Yes, there are teachers who need to leave the classroom because they lack the skills, the interest, or the heart for the challenges of teaching. We do have our deadwood in the teaching profession; and, it is true that if there is even one such, it's one too many because children are too precious to risk.

In the big picture, however, and there are many, many teachers worldwide, so it is indeed a BIG picture—teachers are one of the most highly educated, frequently retrained, and continuously updated work forces on earth. Further, I can visit any school campus anywhere at any time and find dedicated, caring, creative, and sacrificing teachers doing noble and substantive work with kids.

But if I can't blame teachers for the mental malaise of their students, you can't blame the students for being reluctant or resistant to learning, either. While it is true that each individual person must be responsible for his or her own actions, students have had no choice in developing the modern public school where they are sometimes asked to attend to nonsense. "Children will struggle to get out of situations where there is nothing to learn, just as they will struggle to escape from situations where breathing is difficult. Inability to learn is suffocating" (Smith 90). Students also did not create for themselves an educational system where they are sometimes asked to take untenable risks to learn, in a society where their very success is based upon knowing the right answer and always being correct. Children should not be put in the position of having to do things that diminish them in their own eyes or in the eyes of those they value because this acts as a threat to their survival as a person (Caine and Caine 139).

And if I can't blame teachers or students for the lack of student achievement in school, I can't blame their parents, either. Parents are not present at the school house with their children everyday; and parents can't force their own children or any other autonomous human being to do what he or she should do, anyway. Besides, parents are human—they are not perfect. Parents struggle like every other human being; in some sense, each of us has a flaw and could be labeled dysfunctional. Further, dysfunction in families, in and of itself, does not take into account the other powerful factors that influence our children like " ...the crime rate, the poverty, and the sleazy values of the mass culture and our drug-and-alcohol-fueled life styles" (Pipher 252). Sometimes these outside influences are more potently at work in the lives of children than their parents are. Even strong families have trouble combating the external stresses that cause " ...hecticness, instability, and inconsistency of daily family life ..." (Goleman 234). In the face of all of this, parents must " ...be gentle with themselves. Parents can only do so much, and they are not responsible for everything"

(Pipher 289).

And so on and on down the list of likely culprits I go, finding places to condemn and places to excuse and ending up in a circular argument with no end. The difficulty with addressing the disengagement of students is the emotional load that parents carry with them when they examine anything that profoundly affects their offspring. Everywhere in nature I see the parents or the pack fight desperately for the children. It is natural to try to find something to blame so that I can have something to fix.

Children are the future; and as such, it becomes *Everyone's* responsibility to do what they can as best they can to nudge them back towards full and happy engagement in what should be the best time of their lives. "Adolescence is a border between adulthood and childhood, and as such it has a richness and a diversity unmatched by any other life stage" (Pipher 52). Childhood is too unique a time to squander.

Nudge to Connection

It has been my great joy to use my daughter's two 4-H Project horses to start other youngsters on horseback. One young girl also started school the year we worked together. One day early in September I asked her how school was going, fully expecting a positive reply. I was shocked, however, when she vehemently answered, "I hate it! All I do is papers, papers, papers!" Her mother confirmed that it was standard operating procedure for this child to bring ten to fifteen worksheets home every night for homework.

I am still aghast at this revelation. I knew that as students progressed through school, began to rotate into different classes with different teachers, and began to be in larger and more impersonal classes that all this created the ingredients and tendencies for those students to feel isolated, turned off, tuned out, and shut down as learners; but I never imagined that the downward spiral could begin in first grade!

Society somehow treats childhood as *preparation for life*; it wants to hurry children to perform and be little adults. *Childhood is life.* All of us who have the power and influence of age and experience should be about putting the child back into the place where children spend that magical portion of their lives—the thirteen or so years, roughly 4,576 days or 109,764 hours.

Schools top to bottom need to spend time figuring out how to invest personal, individual attention in each child, spending "less time ranking children and more time helping them to identify their natural competencies and gifts . . .[finding the] hundreds and hundreds of ways to succeed, and many, many different abilities that will help [them] get there" (Goleman 37).

All schools need to pay attention and implement the ideas repeated in study after study in the exploding volume of brain research that reinforces over and over basic tenets such as:

- Focus on areas of interest (Caine and Caine 131);
- Provide a sense of safety—mental, emotional and physical levels (Caine and Caine 140);
- Give them the ability to also learn about themselves as people (Caine and Caine 157);
- Give them time to reflect on their learning (Caine and Caine 158);
- Enrich like crazy (Jensen 40).

All adults need to insist on a slow down of the meltdown of children's time. Some of my students have schedules that would rival the most high-powered executives in the world. They are over-scheduled. The converse is also true: some children have nothing to do and fill their time with television, video, and computer technology. At the very least, this gives them "a narrow and unrealistic view of the world" (Probst 178); at the worst, it seems to promote an inability to separate reality from make-believe.

The disengagement of students can lead to their ultimate disenfranchisement as productive human beings. Some rare, strong individuals seem to shake off the malaise as they mature; some seem simply to be able to pull themselves out of it by their own bootstraps. It may be no one single person's fault, but it is travesty nonetheless and deserves our best and brightest efforts to stop.

My nudge for now: do more to try to find out how to encourage more and deeper engagement from school children. Try to make instruction more hands-on, more experiential, and more fun. Eliminate threat and build spirits, rather than try to break them. Enjoy the life and energy of childhood instead of trying to suppress it.

Nudge to Hopefulness

I can remember becoming an ecologist in college, participating in organic community gardening, changing from aerosol sprays to pump sprays, and disdaining many people's tendencies toward consumerism/commercialism.

We were living through the days of the Cold War and Vietnam, and we began to see what could happen to many of our friends and acquaintances when they became disillusioned, lost sight of their goals, lacked purpose or direction in life, and lost their hope for their future.

My students now are the children and grandchildren of those turbulent years of change; and further, my students have recently lived through unknowns like Y 2 K. I wonder how each of them felt going to bed December 31, 1999? I wonder if there had been a sense of panic in those around them, stockpiling water and candles and generators and camping equipment in case life as they knew it vanished while they slept? Like Jane Eyre who told Mr. Brocklehurst that she wouldn't die, then, in order to avoid going "where bad children go," I wonder how many childish psychologies decided that they would simply stave off the end of the world by not going to sleep that night? If the world is out of control and children lose hope, then they begin to just want to get things finished and forgotten instead of looked forward to and planned for.

It seems to me that most students come to my class these days more in the sense that they are doing time instead of having the time of their lives. Having fun and limiting threat are certainly cures for some of that, but the problem is always deeper and more complex that we think. So I want also to help children work on other factors that predict future success and direction for life—things like: " . . .being self-assured and interested . . .knowing what kind of behavior is expected and how to rein in the impulse to misbehave . . .being able to wait, to follow directions . . .turn to teachers for help . . .expressing needs while getting along with other children" (Goleman 193), talking about the kind of people they want to be, and setting goals.

I use literature to instill optimism and hope in my students; the human spirit at its best is widely reflected in literature. I make sure to call attention to it. I target instruction in my class as the means students can use to accomplish their goals and hold open their own doors of opportunity. I design my lessons so that they include the important, for always skills.

Sometimes it is in the smallest things that it is possible to give a measure of hopefulness back to students. Take shopping for school supplies, for instance. By the middle school years, my own children knew most of their personal preferences for supplies, and they would call their friends beforehand and settle on all the cool, must-have things; but I knew we would still make a mad dash to the stores the first evening because the children were changing classes for the first time and each teacher would have a list of required spirals, folders, pens, pencils and subject-specific supplies. These rituals of preparing for the start of school added so much fun and heightened the anticipation for my own children; I think it made them ready and excited to learn and feeling confident of their ability to succeed.

By the high school years, however, this joy and confidence has often eroded for many students; and I think, frequently, their parents are so tired after their day's work and the long commute that it is just easier to put off supply shopping until the weekend. Whatever the reasons, it is not uncommon for students to come into my classroom with not even a pencil or a piece of paper.

I could let this scenario be discouraging or disheartening, but I choose to not let it stop any student from participating. Success in school is absolutely dependent upon the tone of the classroom, and that is true whether you are teaching perfect little students or perfect little stinkers. Each child must be accepted where they are, and each of us teachers must cultivate our gardens of positive reactions instead of negative ones.

Janet Allen puts it this way, "If I hoped to help these students become better readers and writers, I had to show them how to get access to the system. In terms of literacy, I believed that access would come with seeing themselves as learners and sharing in the control of their learning" (Allen 46).

I want students to be able to choose the shape and type of supplies they want to use for the work in my class, but I do not want the lack of supplies to be the excuse for students not to access the system. If I draw a line immediately that a student is either responsible or irresponsible—whether I voice that opinion or say it only to myself—I may predispose, by my spoken or so-often-obvious-unspoken expectations, that a student will bloom or wither in my class.

I believe teachers have incredible influence with kids, the climate in the classroom, and the attitudes of the individual learners. I also believe teachers have the obligation and calling to nudge those students toward independent learning and self-direction.

Nudge toward safe thrills

It seems to me that the vast majority of public school students these days have no access to cheap and safe thrills. I'm talking about the kinds of experiences that make the heart beat faster and causes me to think about the steps I must implement to survive. Everybody needs them; they're part of pushing the envelope and learning the hard way. We used to call them rites of passage. Sometimes they were rough passages, too, because life usually gives the test first and the lesson afterwards; but, they always resulted in learning. Rarely does the learner make the same mistakes twice.

There are so many things that kids can't do nowadays because they're liable to get arrested or injured. Gone are the days when they could roam the open places or walk around cities. People now rarely allow others to explore on their private property; and cities, if not overtly unsafe, harbor abductors and other kinds of hidden, shadowy, surreptitious crimes.

The job of parents, then, has become to control and orchestrate every single moment of their children's lives. Is it any wonder that as those confined, guarded, controlled children grow up and try to assert their independence, that they try to assert themselves as far away from adult supervision as they can? And usually they are traveling too fast and engaging or planning the kinds of reckless behaviors that have frightening and long-lasting consequences. The S.A.D. behaviors—sex, alcohol, and drugs.

Organized sports provide the natural highs I am talking about, but they serve an elite and limited group of kids. What about those kids who are less athletically gifted or who are gifted but are cut from teams because of a late start, or politics, or socio-economic conditions? What about those kids caught in a cycle of academic failure whose achievement keeps them cycling on and off the teams that hold all their hopes and dreams?

Every school, especially the ones that field a highly groomed, competitive, championship team year after year, needs a comprehensive intramural sports program. Further, schools need to be helped to be able to provide alternative sports activities like rock climbing, canoeing, scuba diving, backpacking, and horseback riding. Why can't schools underwrite Outward Bound-type programs for any child who would like to participate?

Parents need to look for family activities that involve physical activity and getting out into the great outdoors—maybe bicycling or camping.

Social and governing institutions need to establish think tanks and underwrite the research and development of things for kids to do, things that require the heart to beat a little faster and one's courage to be called out. In the absence of places to take chances in relative safety, kids will simply create their own thrills. The present big three favorites can shorten or rob the indulgers of the joy in the rest of their lives.

The nudge here is simply that taking some chances is either a biological need left over from our cave man days or simply a normal impulse of youth. The natural world can be a terrific tutor for getting students through the times when they must simply put themselves to the challenge as well as the times when they are simply too dumb to know any better. While no one solution is viable for every child, there is still the need to understand this need for passages for every child so each child reaps the benefits of the self-knowledge, confidence, and resiliency resulting from such experiences.

Nudge towards moral decency

In *To Kill a Mockingbird*, it is only the children who cry at the various vicious prejudices that unfold within the story. Something happens to us children as we grow up and leave childhood behind; we see so many awful injustices and cruel behaviors that soon we find ourselves barely flinching at the worst of the worst.

Something needs to be done, and the nudge for us on this issue has to go to us individually, in our families, in our governments, in our churches, in our social organizations, in our media—in short, in any and all of our collective situations. I tell my students every year that I subscribe to the theory of garbage in/garbage out. We are what we consume. And we are not going to consume cruelty or vulgarity in my classroom.

I realize and guard the idea that we have freedom in this country, but the price we are paying for our anything goes attitude is exacting a toll I'm not sure we are willing to pay. It seems to me that we have substituted looks and accouterments for character. We have children who don't know how to make and maintain a friendship or establish a committed relationship. We have girls who would rather be "nice" than "be themselves" (Pipher 39). We have boys who "live with fear in this culture of cruelty" (Kindlon and Thompson 75) and keep the code of silence because "to remain silent is strong and masculine" (Kindlon and Thompson 92). We have adults who are too self-absorbed to notice any of this.

I am not advocating government control or radical intervention. I am calling out only that each of us stand up for ourselves and ours and those we can influence for a more wholesome life. Refusing to patronize that which undermines morality and decency would drive some of it out of business.

Miscellaneous nudges

- Especially in the language arts, I need to teach students the subject matter and skills, but I also need to blend in "lessons on feelings and relationships (Rosenblatt 40). I need to teach students to believe in themselves (Burke 104).
- Systems need to stop over-testing students, which asks them only to look to someone else for final judgments (Probst 224).
- Kids need to get involved in *service to others* to counterbalance a fixation on self.
- Every child needs an investment of time and attention.
- Adults need to show children how to set, work toward, and achieve their goals.
- Adults need to model for children some useful ways to deal with stress, disappointment, or failure.
- Parents need to "trust that teachers can teach and that children will learn if both are given reasonable autonomy" (Smith x).
- Teachers need to heed the "gentle wisdom" in *Horse Sense for People*'s chapters: establishing better communication, taking a stand against violence, operating from trust, the need for safety, allowing choice and the desire to change (Roberts). Here's a taste why:

"It's not the great trainer who can cause his horse to perform. The great trainer can cause a horse to want to perform" (Roberts xxii).

"If he's about the learn, stay out of his way. If all learning is zero through ten, then the most important part of learning is zero through one" (Roberts xxii).

"Keep it simple. Simple is best" (Roberts xxii).

"Learning empirically is essential to achieving wisdom" (Roberts 95).

———————————————

WORKS CITED

Burke, Jim. *Reading Reminders*. Portsmouth, NH: Boynton/Cook Publishers, 2000.

Caine, Renate Nummela and Geoffrey Caine. *Making Connections*. New York: Innovative Learning Publications, 1991.

Goleman, Daniel. *Emotional Intelligence*. New York: Bantam Books, 1995.

Jensen, Eric. *Teaching with The Brain in Mind*. Alexandria, Virginia: Association for Supervision and Curriculum Development, 1998.

Kindlon, Dan and Michael Thompson. *Raising Cain*. New York: Ballantine Books, 1999.

Pipher, Mary, Ph.D. *Reviving Ophelia*. New York: Ballantine Books, 1994.

Probst, Robert E. *Response and Analysis: Teaching Literature in Jr. & Sr. High School*. Portsmouth, NH: Heinemann, 1988.

Roberts, Monty. *Horse Sense for People*. New York: Viking, 2001.

Rosenblatt, Louise. *The Reader, the Text, the Poem*. Carbondale: Southern Illinois University Press, 1978.

Smith, Frank. *Reading Without Nonsense*. New York: Teacher's College Press, 1985.

The Seventh Nudge

THE SEVENTH NUDGE

The Story

When I first learned about picture books, I'm afraid I purchased them mostly by looks. Lucky for me, many good picture books are well-marketed by their covers! Now I spend hours three or four times per year in children's bookstores, reading the books thoroughly and deciding how, or if, I can use the new possibilities instructionally. I also have good friends who own bookstores and who keep me apprised of the newest and best. The books I purchase now have to work hard (or else they have to be just right for my two little grandsons.) Books I choose for my classroom also usually have limited text. I own a number of books of longer stories, but I tend not to use them in the classroom unless they are simply perfect for a lesson. Since I try to keep a sense of movement in the classroom and teach in chunks, shorter books fit better into my class rhythm. There is always so much to do in any given period; students need their sustained time for taking the lessons and working on the craft: reading and writing.

Many students pick up the trade books I read aloud and read them again themselves. Picture books, often called trade books, are such an important part of the work I do with students in the classroom that many of my friends suggested that the best way I could nudge anyone who might peruse this modest volume was to compile an annotated list of a few of my favorite books. While I have not attempted to alphabetize or prioritize this list in the order of importance or favor, what I have done is to put some books into general categories or topic/genre groups and write a brief note as to each one's place in my thinking or an overall statement as to a particular category's use. I hope this will be useful to you.

Poetry Possibilities

1. George, Jean Craighead. *To Climb a Waterfall.* New York: Philomel Books, 1995.

Use this one because of the science: waterfalls, trout streams, salamanders, Water pennies, and hemlock. The vocabulary is also instructive: *freshet,* and *caddis fly youngster.*

2. Appelt, Kathi. *Bat Jamboree.* New York: Morrow Junior Books, 1996.

Fun nostalgia for drive-in movies. Great ending play on words: "till the bat lady sings."

3. Kipling, Rudyard edited by Eileen Gillooly. *Poetry for Young People.* New York: Sterling Publishing Company, Inc., 2000.

"The Thousandth Man"
"If"
"Natural Theology"

Because of the times in which we live, these are poems that need to be read to students.

4. Vozar, David. *Yo, Hungry Wolf!* New York: Doubleday, 1993.

The best book for teaching writing off the text from a nursery rhyme—plus marvelous rhythm and a good model for dialogue in poetry. This book is just plain fun to read out loud!

5. Esbensen, Barbara Juster. *Dance With Me.* New York: HarperCollins Publishers, 1995.

Get some 'bubbles" (craft stores sell individual bottles for weddings that are relatively inexpensive) and various bubble wands, blow bubbles about the room and read "Bubbles."

These are great nature poems with wonderful illustrations for lightning, wind, tide, rain, among others.

6. Esbensen, Barbara Juster. *Echoes for the Eye.* New York: HarperCollins Publishers, 1996.

These poems are about patterns in nature—how perfect, since the brain loves patterns. This is a great book to connect to students' prior knowledge.

7. Florian, Douglas. *Insectlopedia.* San Diego: Harcourt Brace & Company, 1998.

Great fun poems. Gives inspiration and simple ideas for writing.
Word choice: "Daddy Longlegs"
Rhythm: "The Army Ants"
Shape: "The Inchworm"

8. Janeczko, Paul B. *Home on the Range.* New York: Dial Books, 1997.

Cowboy poetry, but elevates the perception many students will have about the topic. "To Be a Top Hand" teaches that learning is an important part of everyone's living.

9. Mullins, Patricia. *One Horse Waiting for Me.* New York: Simon & Schuster, 1998.

A counting book, but the art is created from torn scraps of paper, and the book must be shared for that reason if none other. Further, many children like horses and can make connections with rocking horses, sea horses, and carousels.

10. Chandra, Deborah. *Balloons and Other Poems.* Canada: HarperCollins Canada, Ltd., 1990.

Let kids write poems on balloons and blow them up. These poems are easy teaches for any of the comparative devices in poetry: personification, simile, and metaphor.

11. Greenfield, Eloise. *Honey, I Love.* New York: Harper Trophy, 1986.

Great poems to use in association with the Quicklist. "Way Down in the Music" will ring true with kids for the power music has in their lives. Jump rope in class while reading "Rope Rhymes." (Get fifteen feet of one of those heavy grass ropes and just swing it back and forth—not overhead.) "Things" speaks to the permanence of writing and gives an example of repetition.

12. Schertle, Alice. *A Lucky Thing.* San Diego: Browndeer Press, 1999.

A book about writing poems—pastoral and nature themes—beautiful art—clever word choice—free verse.

13. Paulsen, Gary. *Canoe Days.* New York: Doubleday, 1999.

Snapshots of peace and quiet. A feast for all auditory and visual senses.

14. Adoff, Arnold. *Outside Inside Poems.* San Diego: Voyager Books, 1995.

Used to teach perspective, point of view, zooming in and zooming out.

15. Rosen, Michael J. *All Eyes on the Pond.* New York: Hyperion, 1994.

Unique, captivating word choice and illustrations. Useful for teaching perspective. I like the imagery in this book.

16. Harley, Avis. *Fly With Poetry.* Honesdale, Pennsylvania: Wordsong/Boyds Mills Press, 2000.

"...introduces a rich variety of poetic forms and techniques." I like the departure from the usual fare. There are some new and different poems and terms in here to expand the knowledge of students.

17. Goldstein, Bobbye S., (Ed.). *Inner Chimes.* Honesdale, Pennsylvania: Wordsong/Boyds Mills Press, 1992.

Poems about poetry and poetry writing—invaluable.

18. Pratt, Kristin Joy. *A Fly in the Sky.* Nevada City, CA: Dawn Publications, 1996.

—_____. *A Swim through the Sea.* Nevada City, CA: Dawn Publications, 1994.

This pair of books is just the best for beautiful illustrations, unique creatures, and great alliteration. Further, what an encouragement to student writers that Pratt wrote and published these books at a very young age!

Mythology, The Odyssey, Legend, Fairy Tale Possibilities

1. Fisher, Leonard Everett. *Cyclops.* New York: Holiday House, 1991.

The giant story from the *Odyssey;* fine graphics—a good book for visualizing.

2. DePaola, Tomie. *The Legend of the Bluebonnet.* New York: G.P. Putnam's Sons, 1983.

The retelling of an old Texas myth, this is a precious tale of unselfishness that is important for our times.

3. Yolen, Jane. *Wings.* San Diego: Harcourt Brace Jovanovich, Publishers, 1991.

The story of Daedalus and Icarus in a truly beautiful visual presentation.

4. Wisniewski, David. *Sundiata.* New York: Clarion Books, 1992.

A story told from the oral tradition of African *griots*. Wisniewski always gives a full page of historical information at the end of the story.

5. Wisniewski, David. *Golem.* New York: Clarion Books, 1996.

An introduction to Jewish culture and thought; this is a good teaser for *The Chosen* by Chaim Potok.

6. Lewis, Paul Owen. *Storm Boy.* Hillsboro, Oregon: Beyond Words Publishing, Inc., 1995.

Follows the mythic traditions of the Pacific Northwest Coast Indians. I use this as an introduction to *I Heard the Owl Call My Name* by Margaret Craven. Further, the inside back pages of the book offer insight into several motifs indigent to these peoples.

7. MacGill-Callahan, Sheila. *The Children of Lir.* New York: Dial Books, 1993.

This is an Irish legend believed to be the basis for Shakespeare's *King Lear*. It is also a sort of *Snow White* tale because the children are the victims of an evil stepmother.

8. McLerran, Alice. *The Ghost Dance.* New York: Clarion Books, 1995.

This book weaves together historical fact and Native people beliefs; I think it is important for students because it is a call to responsible care for the Earth.

9. Olson, Dennis L. *Special Gifts*. Minnetonka, Minnesota: NorthWood Press, 1999.

Based on a Lakota Indian year-round tale, this book is about human qualities that need to be read about, discussed, and held up as personal goals for all peoples: love and honor.

10. Celsi, Teresa. *The Fourth Little Pig*. Austin, Texas: Raintree Steck-Vaughn, Publishers, 1992.

Girls like this book because the fourth pig is female and is much braver than the boys. I use this for the WN to get students thinking about sexual stereotyping.

11. Ketteman, Helen. *Bubba the Cowboy Prince*. New York: Scholastic Press, 1997.

My first-favorite fractured *Cinderella*. Wonderful throughout. A hoot to read out loud; students love the "fairy godcow."

12. Buehner, Caralyn. *Fanny's Dream*. New York: Dial Books For Young Readers, 1996.

This is another Cinderella-type story, but it is really a special one teaching the lessons that beauty is only skin deep and that relationship is built on much more than looks. Important ideas to plant in students' minds.

13. Bruchac, Joseph. *The First Strawberries*. New York: Puffin Books, 1993.

What a sweet book about the power of angry words and how they affect our relationships with those we love.

14. Wolfson, Margaret Olivia. *Marriage of the Rain Goddess*. New York: Marlowe & Company, 1996.

Inspired by a fragment of a Zulu story, this book also asks students to look beyond the surface and the physical for real beauty. Although longer in text than I really like to read in class, this is too beautiful a book to withhold from students.

Idea Books (to help teachers do unique, kooky things in class – no individual comments for these books)

1. Day, Jon. *Let's Make Magic.* New York: Kingfisher Books, 1992.

2. Irvine, Joan. *How to Make Pop-Ups.* New York: Beech Tree Paperback Book, 1987.

3. Schmidt, Norman. *Super Paper Airplanes.* New York: Sterling Publishing Co., Inc., 1996.

4. Norden, Dr. Beth B. *The Bee.* Boston, Massachusetts: Little, Brown and Company, 1991.

5. Mudd, Maria M. *The Butterfly.* Boston, Massachusetts: Little, Brown and Company, 1991.

6. Valenta, Barbara. *Pop-o-Mania.* New York: Dial Books, 1997.

Grammar Books

Use any of the following books by Ruth Heller; published by Putnam and Grosset or Grosset and Dunlap between 1987 and 1998:

>*Up, Up and Away* (adverbs)
>*Merry-Go-Round* (nouns)
>*Many Luscious Lollipops* (adjectives)
>*Kites Sail High* (verbs)
>*A Cache of Jewels* (collective nouns)

Fantastic! Wow! And Unreal!
(interjections and conjunctions)
Behind The Mask (prepositions)

The key to using these books is to use them as introductions, and then have students find them in their reading and find them in their writing. I use these to introduce the more complex constructions of parts of speech—gerunds, infinitives, participles, and clauses.

Sensitivity Training/Problem-Solving Possibilities

1. Jimenez, Francisco. *La Mariposa.* Boston, Massachusetts: Houghton Mifflin Company, 1998.

Based on a true story, this book calls us to understand how difficult it is to move to a place where language and culture are new.

2. Lewis, Kim. *Floss.* Cambridge, Massachusetts: Candlewick Press, 1992.

"All work and no play makes Jack a dull boy." Enough said.

3. Rylant, Cynthia. *Silver Packages.* New York: Orchard Books, 1987.

This book is confirmation of the fact that desire and determination can conquer any obstacles.

4. Baker, Keith. *The Magic Fan.* San Diego: Voyager Books, 1989.

This book lets students know the magic they have is within themselves and not bound by others' thoughts or circumstances.

5. Knowles, Sheena. *Edward the Emu.* Sydney, NSW: Angus & Robertson, 1988.

This is a book about being satisfied with who you are. Fun to read and a favorite of students.

6. Knowles, Sheens. *Edwina the Emu*. New York: HarperTrophy, 1997.

This book is a companion/sequel to the one above, but its message is more that we have to know ourselves and come to realize what is important to us.

7. Myers, Christopher. *Wings*. New York: Scholastic Press, 2000.

A *powerful* book about summoning the courage to be your own true self.

8. Arnold, Tedd. *Parts*. New York: Dial Books, 1997.

I love to read this book out loud. It is a hilarious look about how we can misunderstand the processes of nature, especially those that occur in our own bodies. Students can identify with this at many different ages, so it helps access memory and story for kids.

9. Bahr, Mary. *The Memory Box*. Morton Grove, Illinois: Albert Whitman & Company, 1992.

Many students have grandparents or great-grandparents who are suffering from dementia or Alzheimer's; this book helps explain what it is like and brings some peace and understanding about this condition.

10. Cooper, Helen. *The Bear Under the Stairs*. New York: Dial Books, 1993.

If you have ever imagined something that made you afraid, you will identify with this book. It has some repeated elements that make it stick in the memory and fun to read, as well.

11. Fox, Mem. *Tough Boris*. San Diego, CA: Harcourt Brace & Jovanovich, 1994.

It is perfectly OK for men to cry; even tough guys do it!

12. Gregory, Nan. *How Smudge Came.* Alberta, Canada: Northern Lights Books for Children, Red Deer College Press, 1995.

This is a precious book that handles the subject of people with mental challenges in a tender and loving way. I also love the power that the puppy has in this book to ease the burden of those who normally would not get to hold and cuddle a live dog.

13. Waddell, Martin. *Owl Babies.* Cambridge, Massachusetts: Candlewick Press, 1992.

It is human nature to seek security; this book addresses that idea. Different students will see the type of person they are among the characters of this book.

14. Fox, Mem. *Feathers and Fools.* San Diego: Harcourt Brace & Company, 1989.

This is a powerful book about what prejudice can cause—for birds or for people.

15. Carr, Jan. *The Nature of the Beast.* New York: Tambourine Books, 1996.

This book is so much fun to read aloud that I tell myself that's why I do it; but it is a book that reminds me that children are not little adults, and that I should understand things from their point of view. Please use a beast voice for "SAAAAY LA VEEEEE!"

16. Stanley, Diane. *Saving Sweetness.* New York: G.P. Putnam's Sons, 1996.

Most students don't know what it is like to be orphaned, but they may still identify with this book if they have adults in their lives who don't seem to get it. Besides, kindness is never out of fashion. This book has a sequel—*Raising Sweetness.*

17. Abercrombie, Barbara. *Charlie Anderson.* New York: Aladdin Paperbacks, 1990.

If you have students who are going through the divorce of their parents, this book, or the discussion and writing that may erupt from it, will help them feel better and less alone.

18. Mellonie, Bryan and Robert Ingpen. *Lifetimes*. Toronto: Bantam Books, 1983.

The sub-title of this book is "The beautiful way to explain death to children." I can't add a better endorsement than that.

19. Lindbergh, Reeve. *Grandfather's Lovesong*. New York: Puffin Books, 1993.

The natural world can often be used to help us say what is on our hearts. Beautiful book to open us up to the loving words that need to come out for those around us.

20. Cooke, Trish. *The Grandad Tree*. Cambridge, Massachusetts: Candlewick Press, 2000.

This is another wonderful book that helps us deal with the aging and loss of those we love.

Topical Possibilities for Specific Lessons

Persuasive Writing:

1. Viorst, Judith. *Earrings*. New York: Macmillan Publishing Company, 1993.

2. Grambling, Lois G. *Can I Have a Stegosaurus, Mom? Can I Please?* USA: BridgeWater Books, 1995.

To Encourage Reading

1. Lyon, George Ella. *Book*. New York: DK Publishing, Inc., 1999.

2. Winch, John. *The Old Woman Who Loved to Read.* New York: Holiday House, 1996.

3. Mora, Pat. *Tomas and the Library Lady.* New York: Alfred A. Knopf, 1997.

4. Polacco, Patricia. *The Bee Tree.* New York: Philomel Books, 1993.

5. San Souci, Robert D. *A Weave of Words.* New York: Orchard Books, 1998.

Surprise Endings

1. Essley, Roger. *Appointment.* New York: Green Tiger Press, 1993.

A Memoir

1. Curtis, Jamie Lee. *When I Was Little.* New York: HarperCollins Publishers, 1993.

To Replace Trite (or unacceptable) Language

1. Wood, Audrey and Don. *Elbert's Bad Word.* San Diego: Harcourt Brace & Company, 1988.

To Introduce Grouping Strategies

1. London, Jonathan. *Fire Race.* San Francisco: Chronicle Books, 1993.

To Encourage Curiosity

1. Merriam, Eve. *The Wise Woman and Her Secret.* New York: Simon & Schuster Books, 1991.

For Letter Writing

1. James, Simon. *Dear Mr. Blueberry.* New York: Aladdin, 1991.

2. Spurr, Elizabeth. *The Long, Long Letter.* New York: Hyperion, 1996.

3. Baker, Keith. *The Dove's Letter.* San Diego: Harcourt Brace & Company, 1993.

To Introduce Paragraphing

1. Hunt, Jonathan. *Illuminations.* New York: MacMillan Publishing Company, 1993.

To Introduce Introductions and Conclusions

1. Stevens, Janet. *Tops & Bottoms.* New York: Harcourt Brace & Company, 1996.